The CLASSIFIER'S GUIDE TO LC CLASS H:

Subdivision Techniques for the Social Sciences

by
Lillie D. Caster

Neal-Schuman Publishers, Inc.
New York   London

Published by Neal-Schuman Publishers, Inc.
23 Cornelia Street
New York, New York 10014

Printed and bound in the United States of America.

Library of Congress Cataloging-in-Publication Data

Caster, Lillie C.
  The classifier's guide to LC Class H.

  Bibliography: p.
  Includes index.
  1. Classification--Books--Social Sciences.
2. Classification, Library of Congress. I. Title.
Z696.U5H 1986   025.4'63   85-28459
ISBN 0-918212-99-5

contents

PART THREE   APPENDIX

acknowledgments

It is difficult to express appreciation to all those who gave me help in the preparation of the manuscript for this book. I was most fortunate in having Mary K.D. Pietris, Chief, Subject Cataloging Division, Library of Congress, read the manuscript and contribute her professional knowledge. I was also fortunate in the assistance given me by my former colleagues at North Carolina State University: Ann Smith and Inez Ray for proofreading; Nell L. Waltner and Walter M. High for their thorough reading of the draft and their suggestions; and Audrey Cordes for assuming the drudgery of checking and rechecking the numerous class numbers used in the examples.

I owe a debt of gratitude to Desretta McAllister-Harper and Benjamin Speller, two associates at the School of Library and Information Science, North Carolina Central University, for their encouragement and assistance including the loan of books both personal and from the school's library. A copy of Class H was literally worn out in the search for examples. I am particularly in the debt of Denise Gray for retyping several versions of the work and producing each with admirable accuracy.

Thanks are due to Susan Getty, Edward P. Thompson, and Robert Esposito, friends who were supportive in various ways. A special thanks to my little seven-year-old neighbor, Jeffrey Glenn Harding, who was delighted to help alphabetize the slips for the geographical locations in the Appendix.

Finally, grateful acknowledgment is given to Vivian Halpern. If it had not been for her, the idea for this book may never have come about.

Personal time is at a premium but no one when asked to help denied the request. Good and kind friends, please accept my deep-felt thanks.

Lillie D. Caster

introduction

The Classifier's Guide to LC Class H: Subdivision Techniques for the Social Sciences explains and describes selected techniques of subdivision as they occur in one class of the Library of Congress Classification. The book is addressed to students of library and information science, to beginning classifiers, and to librarians who wish to renew their acquaintance with the Classification. It is intended to be an aid in developing the skills necessary for becoming proficient in the application of Classification.

There are three main reasons for focusing on Class H. First, it is often chosen as the introductory class in library school cataloging courses. This is attributable to the extensive use of tables within the schedule and to the ten auxiliary Tables of Geographical Divisions. Because of the tables, Class H is considered to be one of the more difficult schedules to learn and apply. Second, the fourth and latest edition of Class H (1980-1981), produced in a new format, presents significant revisions in captions, in geographical listings, in tables within the schedule, and in the Tables of Geographical Divisions. In the current literature on the Classification, there are only a few examples from Class H. Of the current literature on Class H, none is based fully on the fourth edition. Third, while there are numerous scope, see, confer, and inclusion notes in the schedule to assist classifiers in the choice of the most appropriate class numbers, there are very few directions for applying subdivision techniques.

The twelve chapters of The Classifier's Guide to LC Class H are organized into two parts. In Part One, Subdivision Techniques, each chapter treats one of the subdivision techniques. The general pattern of each chapter includes introductory descriptions, excerpts from Class H illustrating the forms of the subdivision technique, an "observe" section following each displayed example stating its salient points, and procedures for applying the technique using one of the examples.

Part One would be complete without Chapter 6, General Special; and, it must be pointed out that General Special is not properly a technique of subdivision. But its inclusion seemed justified on the basis of the uncommon juxtaposition of two words directly opposed in meaning. When given as a subdivision without any defining topics, the term is not self-explanatory and requires further elucidation.

Part Two, Geographical Divisions, is an expansion of Chapter 7, Geographical Order. Chapters eight through eleven focus on subdivision techniques for four particular types of geographical areas. In Chapter 12, several types of areas are grouped together. The general pattern of each chapter is similar to that of Part One; however, application procedures are not repeated.

Undergirding the organization of The Classifier's Guide to LC Class H into individual chapters devoted to each technique is the basic idea that explanations, descriptions, and examples scattered in the literature should be brought together in one place. Assemblage in this way provides a unified approach to subdivision techniques. Thus, the book augments and supplements existing works on the Library of Congress Classification.

As used in this book, a subdivision is a word or words denoting a division or aspect of a subject. Caption is used interchangeably with subdivision. The term subdivision techniques is used to indicate methods by which subjects and aspects of subjects are further divided or subarranged. The word subarrangement is an alternative to subdivision technique.

The examples excerpted from the schedule and displayed in the text are intended to be representative. Generally, only that portion of a class directly illustrating a technique is given. Classified lists of geographical divisions have been shortened to only the first few place names. The list of places in Example 6, Chapter 9, Countries, is the exception. In addition to the displayed examples, references are made to other class numbers in the H schedule exemplifying the characteristics of the techniques. Occasionally, related variable notation is explained.

The class numbers of all displayed and quoted examples have been checked against the 1981-1982 Class H volumes of Library of Congress Classification Schedules: A Cumulation of Additions and Changes and in L.C. Classification--Additions and Changes, January, 1983- March, 1984. Significant additions and changes to an example from those sources are incorporated in the text. Changes noted in names of geographical divisions in auxiliary tables and the new name for Underdeveloped areas, Developing countries, apply wherever the former names are listed in the schedule.

The Library of Congress Shelflist, Microfiche Edition, provided verification of usage in a number of instances. Guide card information, names of regions of other countries, subject headings, and catalog entries from the Shelflist are included in appropriate places. Catalog entries have been copied without any updating to conform to current practices.

Two choices in terminology have been made. Author numbers, book numbers, cutter numbers, however called, play an important role in class- and call-number formation. Of the three terms, cutter number has been preferred. Cutter number can be applied to constructions other than book numbers, such as in topical cutter numbers. In the literature on the

Classification, cutter number, with or without the "C" capitalized, is consistently employed and, in the Classification itself, the phrase "Use successive Cutter numbers" occurs as an instruction. In the procedural examples, cutter numbers have been assigned where they express a part of the class number. Complete call numbers are noted where it seemed desirable. The resulting class or call numbers are hypothetical in that they bear no relationship to any one shelf list.

Main entry, the second choice in terms, is used as the commonly accepted heading for a basic catalog entry. The three heading choices -- personal author, corporate body, title -- are covered by the term. While there has been reduced emphasis on main entry in the Anglo-American Cataloguing Rules, Second Edition, and while computer manipulation may make the term obsolete, the concept of main entry is still a viable one at present.

The scope of The Classifier's Guide to LC Class H has been defined as subdivision techniques. Accordingly, the book does not deal with the history and development of the Library of Congress Classification, its theory, its basic features, structure and format, its advantages or disadvantages. Nor is it concerned with selecting and fitting cutter numbers into shelf lists. These matters have been treated thoroughly in works listed in the bibliography. Generally, too, most of the topics would be prefatory in classroom instruction to the introduction of any one class.

The widespread availability of Library of Congress cataloging copy with assigned Library of Congress Classification call numbers perhaps reduces the need for classifiers; nevertheless, there is hardly a library of any size that does not receive material for which cataloging copy is not available. The general reclassification to the Library of Congress system of the 1960s and 1970s augurs well for its continued use by libraries. The Classifier's Guide to LC Class H will have achieved its aims if the unified, detailed explanations of subdivision techniques in one class assists in developing proficiency in applying the Classification. It is essential that the user have in hand both volumes of Class H.

S.R. Ranganathan, the eminent Indian librarian, states as his first law of library science that books are for use. It is hoped that those for whom this book is intended will find it useful.

part one
subdivision techniques

chapter 1
alphabetical order/
non-alphabetical order

The antithetical topics, alphabetical order and non-alphabetical order are discussed in the same chapter precisely because they are opposites. Alphabetical subarrangements are mnemonic; nonalphabetical subarrangements are not. Conversely, the two topics have in common subordination to a single class number and the prescriptive nature of their instructions. The instruction to alphabetize, A-Z, and the instruction not to alphabetize (not A-Z), follow immediately after the caption.

ALPHABETICAL ORDER OF TOPICS

Alphabetical order is used "when a systematic sequence of coordinate subdivisions cannot be discerned" and occasionally when there is a shortage of whole numbers.[1] Alphabetical order specifies and subarranges elements that would otherwise fall at random into a general class.[2] The alphabetical instruction requires cutter numbers to be derived from the initial letters of the topics named in the captions. The cutter numbers thus derived are aptly called topical cutter numbers. Each topical cutter number becomes a part of the class number to which it is assigned in a call number.

Depending upon the subject, a caption may name companies, products, places, institutions, organizations, industries, etc. Each is a class or group of a particular kind. In numerous instances, the topics with their cutter numbers are enumerated beneath the captions.

Listed Topics

Topical cutter numbers are printed in the schedule when the Library of Congress has works to which the cutter numbers have been applied. New topics are continually being added. An example of a lengthy list supplied in the schedule is at HF5686 (Accounting. Bookkeeping. By business or activity, A-Z). An interesting array is HE6183 (Postage stamps). A short list of four alphabetical topics is shown in Example I.

7

EXAMPLE I

```
                    Railway administration
                 Traffic
                    Rates
                       Passenger tariff
                          Including schedules
HE1951                    General works
    1953                  Adjustable.  Sliding
    1957                  Zone system
                          Reduced rates, commutation rates, etc.
    1959                     General works
    1960                     Rates for special classes of
                                     passengers, A-Z
                             .B5 Blind
                             .C5 Civil Service employees
                             .T6 Tourist
                             .W7 Workingmen
```

OBSERVE

1. One class number is assigned to rates for special classes of passengers.

2. Four special classes of passengers are listed in alphabetical order.

3. Cutter numbers are assigned from the names of each special class.

4. The class numbers for each of the four topics would be:

    HE1960.B5   HE1960.T6
    HE1960.C5   HE1960.W7

Sometimes, the topical cutter numbers are listed at another class number in the schedule. Then, a footnote refers to the appropriate pages. Such a referral is made at HD4966 (Wages. By industry or trade, A-Z).

If it should happen that a particular topic does not appear in the schedule alphabetical display, a cutter number must be derived and inserted in its alphabetical place. In Example I, the topical cutter number could be inserted for senior citizens, an unlisted special class of passengers.

Perhaps the most frequently repeated request for alphabetization occurs for geographical subdivision. Appended tables provide preassigned cutter numbers for regions and countries of the world and for cities and states of the United States. Alphabetical order of geographical divisions is discussed in Chapter 7, Geographical Order.

Internal tables contain alphabetically arranged lists of topics. One such list appears in the table for HN101-942.5 (Social history and conditions), opposite (20).

The topics listed for HD8039 (Labor. By industry or trade), appear to be simply alphabetical topical cutter numbers but according to a footnote example, they are to be treated as successive cutter numbers. The several alphabetical arrays of special products and other items for HD9000-9999 (Special industries and trades) display a slightly different form of preassigned cutter numbers. Spreads of two, three, and four numbers have been assigned to the various products. These are also to be applied successively. The application of the two alphabetical displays is explained in Chapter 4, Successive Cutter Numbers.

Unlisted Topics

When alphabetical order is called for and topics are not listed in the schedule, both the topics and the cutter numbers must be determined. Assistance in the determination of topics to be included is often given in the wording of the caption. On the other hand, captions such as Other, common at the end of classes, are without topical indication in themselves. The clue lies in the preceding subdivisions of the subject. It is helpful when the schedule supplies an inclusion note or an e.g. annotation. Unlike listed topics to which new ones are added as they develop, no further indication of topics will be provided when an e.g. note is printed. The examples show several different forms of captions.

EXAMPLE 2

```
                    Criminology
                        Criminal classes
                            Biography
        HV6245                  Collective
           6248                 Individual,  A-Z
```

OBSERVE

1. One class number is assigned to Individual, A-Z.
2. Names of the individuals are lacking.
3. Criminal classes and Biography are the clues to the meaning of Individual.
4. A-Z after Individual requires first cutter numbers to represent the surnames of the biographees.

EXAMPLE 3

	Agricultural associations, societies, etc.
HD1483	General works
	By region or country
	United States
1484	General works
1485	By society, A-Z

OBSERVE

1. The caption states specifically that the topics are to be the names of societies.

2. The societies to be cuttered are not listed.

3. The societies are limited to one kind and one country.

EXAMPLE 4

	Postal service
	International postal service
	General works
	Universal Postal Union
HE 6251	Periodicals. Serials
6261	General works
6271	General special
	Pan American Postal Union
6275	Periodicals. Serials
6276	General works
6277	General special
6278	Other unions, A-Z
	e.g. .A4 African Postal Union

OBSERVE

1. Other unions, A-Z, excludes the two unions named at HE6251+ and HE6275+.

2. The word union qualifies Other.

3. HE6278 is annotated to show the topical cutter number and name of one union to be included.

EXAMPLE 5

Air transportation
    Periodicals. Serials. By language

HE 9761	Polyglot
.1	English
.2	French
.3	German
.4	Russian and other Slavic
.5	Spanish and Portuguese
.6	Arabic
.7	Chinese
.8	Japanese
.9	Other, A-Z

OBSERVE

Languages not accounted for in the preceding subdivisions are to form the alphabetical sequence of topics for HE9761.9

Under subdivisions in internal tables, alphabetical sequences may be called for without providing topical lists or examples. The table for HG8550-8740.5 (Insurance) has subdivisions for Local, A-Z, and By company, A-Z, without any topics listed.

NON-ALPHABETICAL ORDER OF TOPICS

In contrast to alphabetical order, some topics are specifically forbidden to be arranged in alphabetical sequence. The direction not to alphabetize is usually assigned to the subdivisions Other, Other special, and similar combinations at the end of classes. Denial of alphabetical sub-arrangement to subdivisions places them among all the other subdivisions enumerated in the schedule without subarrangement directions. Generally, in the absence of instructions, normal procedure is to complete call numbers with main entry cutter numbers; that is what happens when topical cutter numbers are forbidden. Two examples show (not A-Z).

EXAMPLE 6

Alcoholism. Intemperance. Temperance reform
  Care and rehabilitation of alcoholics
    Including social work

HV 5275	General works
	Practice. Methods of treatment

5276	General works
5277	Keeley cure
5278	Other special treatments (not A-Z)

OBSERVE

1. One method of treatment is assigned an individual class number.

2. Other special at the end of the class provides for treatments which have not been enumerated.

3. Alphabetical subarrangement of other treatments is forbidden.

EXAMPLE 7

Taxation. Administration and procedure
  Other special forms
    Articles of consumption, raw materials, manufactures
      Raw materials

HJ 5751	General works
5754	By region or country, A-Z
	Special materials, see HD, HF, etc.

      Manufactures

5761	General works
5764	By region or country, A-Z
	Special articles, see HD, HF, etc.

      Luxuries
        Cf. HJ4581+, Personal property law

5771	General works
	By region or country
	United States
5773	General works
5774	By region or state, A-Z
5775	Other regions or countries, A-Z
	Special
	Furniture, instruments, vehicles, boats, yachts
5777	General works
5780	Special, A-Z
	.B6 Boats
	.V4 Vehicles
5783	Wearing apparel. Jewelry
	Animals (Pets, etc.)
5788	General works
	Dogs
5791	General and United States
5792	By region or country, A-Z
5793	Horses, etc.

5797	Other (not A-Z) e.g. Amusements, books, club dues, motion pictures, playing cards, servants, soft drinks, theater tickets

OBSERVE

1. Certain special luxuries have been given class numbers in the schedule.

2. A single class number is assigned to Other.

3. Some luxuries for inclusion in Other are arranged alphabetically in a note but cutter numbers are not to be taken from the names of the luxuries.

A third example does not conform to the general rule of assigning book numbers when topical cuttering is prohibited. At HJ2287 (Antiquities. Early forms), the negative direction after Local means to cutter by country rather than main entry. An e.g. note so indicates.

NOTES

1. Charles C. Bead, "The Library of Congress Classification: Development, Characteristics, and Structure," in The Use of the Library of Congress Classification; Proceedings of the Institute on the Use of the Library of Congress Classification, edited by Richard H. Schimmelpfeng and C. Donald Cook (Chicago: American Library Association, 1968), p. 25.

2. Martha L. Manheimer, Cataloging and Classification: A Workbook, 2nd ed. rev. and exp. (New York: Dekker, 1980), p. 80.

chapter 2
dedicated cutter numbers

The term dedicated cutter numbers has been selected for use here but the numbers may be referred to in other sources as "A" and "Z" cutter numbers, as they are called at the Library of Congress; reserved cutter numbers; special-purpose cutter numbers; or official cutter numbers. The assignment of dedicated cutter numbers is described by J. Paul Bain as a technique in which:

> A subdivision is assigned a cutter number that is "dedicated" to that subdivision, which means it cannot be used for the representation of any other meaning than that assigned. Thus periodicals on a given subject are often cuttered .A1, meaning that all periodicals on that given subject will be cuttered .A1 before any other cuttering on title or name is permitted.[1]

Bain also points out the usefulness of the technique:

> "Dedicated cuttering" serves to group together like materials, e.g., "periodicals," usually at the beginning of a sequence of subdivisions. This means that the materials will stand together on the shelves before others of a different type.[2]

Dedicated cuttering is nonmnemonic because the two letters used, A and Z, bear no relationship to the subdivisions to which they are assigned (as they do in alphabetical order). When given in the schedule, the notation must always be used with the class number to which it is assigned.

The notation for dedicated cutter numbers combines the letters A or Z with arabic numbers preceded by a decimal point and followed by the dedicted aspect of the subject. There may be one dedicated number or several. They may or may not be followed by the direction A-Z. If not, cuttering by main entry for the second cutter number is to be understood. A range of dedicated numbers may be assigned to a topic and, in that case, no further cuttering is usually required.

When a dedicated sequence ends, regular cuttering for the next subdivision begins. Digits used in the dedicated series cannot be reused; therefore a limitation is placed on main entries having initial letters of A. If the subdivision for normal cuttering is followed by A-Z, the

A limitation is placed on the cutter number for the topic and the main entry is cuttered without regard to numbers used in the dedicated series.

Some variations in the presentation of dedicated cutter numbers may be seen in the following six examples. The formulation of class numbers with dedicated numbers is explained using Example 2.

EXAMPLE 1

                               Commerce
                                Business
                                  Vocational guidance

HF5381.A1A-Z	Periodicals. Societies. Serials
.A2-Z	General works

OBSERVE

1. There is only one dedicated number: .A1.
2. It is to be assigned as the first cutter number to any of the types of works named in the caption.
3. Alphabetical order for the second cutter number is indicated by A-Z after .A1.
4. For general works, cutter numbers for main entries beginning with A are to be confined to .A2-9.

EXAMPLE 2

                    Waterways
                      By type of waterway
                        Ports, harbors, docks, wharves, etc.
                          North America. United States. Canada

HE 553	General works	
554	By place, A-Z	
	.A3	Atlantic ports
	.A4	Gulf ports
	.A6	Pacific ports
	.A7	River ports
	.A8-Z	Individual ports, A-Z

OBSERVE

1. There are several dedicated cutter numbers.
2. .A1, .A2, and .A5 are unassigned.
3. A-Z does not follow the dedicated numbers.
4. The dedicated sequence ends with .A7.

PROCEDURE

The procedure for forming class numbers is outlined in Example 2 in which types of waterways by place have been assigned to HE554.

HE554
.A3 Atlantic ports

    1.   To any work dealing with the subject, assign the dedicated number as the first cutter number.

    2.   Assign a second cutter number from the main entry.

.A4 Gulf ports

    1.   To any work dealing with the subject, assign the dedicated number as the first cutter number.

    2.   Assign a second cutter number from the main entry.

.A6 Pacific ports

    1.   To any work dealing with the subject, assign the dedicated number as the first cutter number.

    2.   Assign a second cutter number from the main entry.

.A7 River ports

    1.   To any work dealing with the subject, assign the dedicated number as the first cutter number.

    2.   Assign a second cutter number from the main entry.

.A8-Z   Individual ports, A-Z

    1.   To any work dealing with the subject, assign the first cutter number from the name of the subject.

        a.   Cutter subjects whose initial letters are A between .A8-9.

        b.   Cutter subjects whose initial letters are B-Z in the regular way.

    2.   Assign a second cutter number from the main entry.

HE554 call numbers for (1) Pacific ports, (2) an individual port, A cutter number limitation, and (3) an individual port cuttered between B-Z are shown in three shortened catalog entries from The Library of Congress Shelflist:

HE554
.A6U56   United States. Maritime Administration.
        United States seaports: Alaska, Pacific coast, and Hawaii.

HE554
.A87P4   Peat, Marwick, Mitchell and Company.
        The port of Albany.

HE554
.M5S3   Schenker, Eric, 1931-
        The port of Milwaukee; an economic review.

If the dedicated letter is Z, substitute Z for A in following the procedure. At HE5635-5720, a series of dedicated Zs is worked out.

EXAMPLE 3

	Clubs and societies for special classes
	Boys' societies
	Special societies
	Boy scouts
	Boy Scouts of America
HS3313.A1-19	Proceedings, annual reports, etc.
.A3	Constitutions, by-laws of BSA. By date
.A4A-Z	Periodicals. By title
.A5	Jamborees, congresses. By date
.A6-Z5	General works
.Z6A-Z	Leaders and committees
.Z7A-Z	Ranks, offices
.Z8-A-Z	Uniforms, insignia
.Z9A-Z	Awards, etc.
	Including Order of the Arrows and religious awards
.Z95A-Z	Merit badges

OBSERVE

1.   The dedicated sequence includes both A and Z.

2.   .A1-19 is a range of dedicated numbers.

3.   Date of publication completes the call number for works assigned .A3 and .A5.

4.   Main entry cutter numbers for general works must be contained within .A6-Z5.

5.   "By title" after the caption for .A4 means that the third element of the call number is to be the cutter number for the title of the periodical.

6.   The last Z number consists of two digits.

The table of dedicated cutter numbers in Example 4 has been reproduced omitting class numbers and places except for the first class number of the United States. Other geographical divisions have been assigned one, two, or three class numbers in the schedule. The dedicated cutter numbers are assigned to three-number countries. Directions for one- and two-number countries are in a separate paragraph.

EXAMPLE 4

Direct taxes (Special)
Land tax. Real estate tax
By region or country
Under each country (except the United States)
(1) .A1 Periodicals. Societies. Serials
.A29 Collected works (nonserial)
General works
.A6   Early works
.A7-Z Recent works
(2)   Special
.A25   Delinquency
.A27   Exemption
.A3   Forest lands, etc.
.A4   Mobile homes
.A5   Improvement, houses, etc.
.A6   Betterments. Special assessments
(3) .A7-Z States, provinces, etc., A-Z
For countries with <u>two numbers</u> combine (2) and
(3); for countries with <u>one number</u> expand (1)
by: Special, .Z7A-Z; Local, .Z9A-Z.
United States

HJ4181   General works

OBSERVE

1.   Dedicated cutter numbers are assigned to three-number countries as indicated by the parenthesized numbers.

2.   A note explains how to handle two- and one-number countries.

3.   The direction for two-number countries extends subdivision (2) by .A7-Z from subdivision (3).

4.   For one-number countries, the direction expands subdivision (1) by .Z7 and .Z9.

5.   The United States, whose subdivisions have class numbers in the schedule, is not subject to the dedicated cutter numbers.

While most frequently the first cutter number of a call number, dedicated cutter numbers sometimes form the second cutter number. Example 5 is one instance of a dedicated cutter number in a secondary position.

EXAMPLE 5

```
                    Commerce
HF2651                  Tariffs on commodities.  By commodity, A-Z
                          Under each:
                            .xA2     General works
                            .xA3-Z  By region or country, A-Z
                          e.g.         Copper
                            .C78A2    General works
                            .C78A3-Z  By region or country, A-Z
```

OBSERVE

1. The dedicated number is combined with a successive cutter number.

2. The dedicated cutter number follows the cutter numbers.

3. A decimal is not used before the dedicated cutter number.

4. An example for one commodity is given.

    a. The first cutter number is for the commodity, as called for by the class caption.

    b. The dedicated cutter number is placed after the commodity cutter number in the call number of a general work.

    c. Regions and countries must be cuttered between .A3-Z.

EXAMPLE 6

```
                    Transportation and communication
                       Passenger traffic (General)
                          By region or country
HE215-300                   Other regions or countries.  Table I[1]
                          Under each country:
                            .A1A-Z General works
                            .A3A-Z Ancient
                            .A5A-Z Medieval
                            .A7-Z5 Modern
                            .Z7A-Z Local
```

1. For Table I, see pp. 331-340 in H-HJ. Add country number in table to 200.

OBSERVE

1. The caption Other regions or countries indicates that some regions or countries have been given prior treatment in the schedule, in this case, America and the United States.

2. Following the caption, Table I of the Tables of Geographical Divisions is quoted.

3. The regions and countries will be found in the central column of the Tables.

4.   Subdivisions of the subject are represented by dedicated cutter numbers under country numbers.

To form a class number for Example 6, an additional step must be taken before attaching the dedicated cutter number. The step is made necessary by the citation of a Table of Geographical Divisions from which a number for the appropriate country is obtained. That country number is then added to the number in the footnote, in this case 200. The dedicated cutter number is attached to the number resulting from the addition. Turkey is 68.25 in Table I. That number and 200 total 268.25. The class number for passenger traffic in ancient Turkey would be HE268.25.A3.

The Table of Regions in the United States appended to the schedule is an excellent example of dedicated cutter numbers. Twenty regions have been assigned the span .A1-195. The subdivisions following under each statement for Other countries preceding HJ12 (Public finance. Documents) have dedicated cutter number spans of approximately 100 each.

Dedicated cutter numbers are standard in one-number range columns of internal tables. Range columns with headings greater than one number may also include dedicated cutter numbers as the table in Example 7 illustrates.

EXAMPLE 7

HG9010-9200.5

Life insurance
   By region or country
      Other regions or countries.   Table VI[1]
      Under each country:

5 nos.		2 nos.	1 no.	
(1)		(1) .A1-4	.A1-3	Periodicals. Serials
(2)		.A4	.A4A-Z	Societies
(3)		.A6	.A5A-Z	Directories
(4)		.A7-Z7	.A6-Z5	General works. History. Statistics
	.Z9	.Z9	.Z6A-Z	Policy
(5)		(2)	.Z7A-Z	Local, A-Z
	.Z9	.Z9	.Z9A-Z	By company, A-Z

---

1.   For Table VI, see pp. 331-340 in H-HJ. Add country number in table to 9000.

OBSERVE

1.   In the 1 no. range column, dedicated cutter numbers are assigned to the subdivisions.

2.   Dedicated cutter numbers in the 5 nos. and 2 nos. columns denote some subdivisions.

NOTES

1.   J. Paul Bain, "The Use of the Tables in the Library of Congress Classification," in Mildred H. Downing, Introduction to Cataloging and Classification, 5th ed. (Jefferson, N.C.: McFarland and Co., 1981), p. 117.

2.   Ibid.

chapter 3
subarranged like

The note "Subarranged like" is a frequent one. Occasionally, "Divided like" or other variations may be used. Whatever the phraseology, the words with their class numbers prescribe the subdivisions and their order for the subject under which they appear. Leo LaMontagne describes Divided like notes as subdivisions provided under some subjects which serve as tables for the subdivision of similar or related topics.[1]   Common subdivisions enumerated only once save space.

There are two sets of numbers where Subarranged like is involved: those to be subarranged and those in the Subarranged like note. The latter will be referred to as the model. The Subarranged like note, printed beneath the subdivision for the class numbers to be subdivided, includes the model numbers. Both sets of numbers are usually in the same subclass as the examples show. The examples, in addition, present some different types of models.

EXAMPLE I

Mathematical economics.   Quantitative methods.
General works, treatises, textbooks
Medieval period, <u>see</u> HB79
Before Adam Smith to 1776/1789

	HB 151	English and American
	153	French
Model	155	German
	157	Italian
	159	Other languages
	161-169	Classical period, 1776/1789 - 1843/1876
		Subarranged like HB151+

OBSERVE

1.   The instruction to subarrange is printed immediately beneath the caption.

2.   The model, appearing immediately above the topic to be subdivided, has one class number for each subdivision.

3.　The plus sign after HB151 in the note indicates that there are additional numbers in the model.

4.　The class number range to be divided and the model number range match each other.

EXAMPLE 2

HB2591-2787　　Demography.　Vital events
Professions.　Occupations
By region or country.　Table II¹
Subarrange each country like HB911-1107

1.　For Table II, <u>see</u> pp. 331-340 in H-HJ.　Add number in table to 2590 or 3500 as the case requires.

Model　HB911-1107　　Births.　Fertility
By region or country.　Table II¹
Under each country:

	2 nos.	1 no.	
(1)		.A3A-Z	General works
(2)		.A5-Z	Local, A-Z

1.　For Table II, <u>see</u> pp. 331-340 in H-HJ.　Add number in table to 910 or 1120 as the case requires.

OBSERVE

1.　An internal table presents the subdivisions in the model.

2.　The example class number span and that of the model equal each other.

3.　Table II of the Tables of Geographical Divisions applies to both the example and the model.

4.　The model and the example are in the same subclass, HB.

EXAMPLE 3

Model	Example
Freemasons 　Societies admitting 　Masons only.　"Side 　degrees"	Odd Fellows 　Oddfellowship among Blacks

EXAMPLE 3, continued
_____

HS 835	Mystic shrine	HS1175	Household of Ruth

HS 835   Mystic shrine   HS1175 Household of Ruth
                                               Subdivided like HS835

    .1   Periodicals. Societies   .1
                Serials
    .3   History   .3
    .4   Law and legislation   .4
    .5   Rituals, etc.   .5
                By region or country
                  United States
    .6   General works   .6
                  .A2 Proceedings
    .7   By state, A-W   .7
                  .A2 Proceedings
    .8   By city, A-Z   .8
                Under each:
                    .x General works
                    .x2 By temple, A-Z
    .9   Other regions and
                countries, A-Z   .9
                Under each country:
                .x General works
                .x2 Local, A-Z

OBSERVE
_____

1.   Subarrangement in the model is by decimal extension of the class number.

2.   The subdivisions and decimal extensions are the same for HS1175 and HS835.

3.   Some subdivisions are further subarranged by dedicated or successive cutter numbers.

_____

EXAMPLE 4
_____

                            Public finance
                              Revenue. Taxation
                                by region or country
                                  Europe
                                    Northern Ireland
HJ2623.A1A-Z   General works
                                History. By periods
Model   .A3A-Z   Early through 1970
        .A5A-Z   1701-1900
        .A7-Z4   1901-
        .Z5A-Z   Special
        2624   Scotland
                          Subarranged like HJ2623
        2625   Wales
                          Subarranged like HJ2623

EXAMPLE 4, continued
_____

OBSERVE

1.   The model is printed before the places to be subdivided by its provisions.
2.   Subdivision in the model is developed by dedicated cutter numbers.
3.   Scotland and Wales each have one class number as does the model.

_____

PROCEDURE

The technique of subarranged like is one of matching the class numbers to be subdivided with the numbers in the model.

1.   Determine the topic or aspect treated in the work.
2.   Match the class numbers to be subdivided with the numbers in the model.
3.   Select the class number opposite the model number which corresponds to the topic treated.

For Example 1, the class numbers corresponding to the model numbers would be:

HB161   HB163   HB165   HB167   HB169

An Italian textbook of the Classical period on the subject would be assigned HB167 to match HB157 of the model. In Example 3, the notations, printed in parallel columns, further illustrate the technique. Attach main entry cutter numbers unless other devices are to be considered first.

In Example 4, the dedicated cutter numbers in the model must be applied before cuttering by main entry. Applying dedicated cutter numbers is discussed in Chapter 2, Dedicated cutter numbers.

In the case of Example 2 where there is a range of class numbers and a reference to a Table of Geographical Divisions, the class number must be determined before sequential numbers (1) and (2) in the internal table of the model can be applied. The procedure for combining a Table of Geographical Divisions with an internal table to form class numbers is presented in Chapter 7, Geographical Order.

A Subarranged like note accompanies the class number range HJ9015-9099.6 (Local finance. Documents) where no countries are listed. The model class numbers, HJ15-99 (Public finance. Documents), present a classified list of geographical divisions with class numbers assigned to each. The countries for HJ9015-9099.6 are to be represented in class numbers by the digits assigned to the places enumerated between HJ15-99. The two sets of class numbers would be matched thus:

for Mexico	HJ15	HJ9015
for Jamaica	HJ27.3	HJ9027.3
for Senegal	HJ85.7	HJ9085.7

One other point about Subarranged like is that the notice may be given in a footnote. That is true for Mexico at HJ4123 (Direct taxes (Special)).

NOTES

1.   Leo E. LaMontagne, American Library Classification with Special Reference to the Library of Congress Classification (Hamden, Conn.: Shoe String Press, 1961), p. 282.

chapter 4
successive cutter numbers

Sequences of the same cutter number with decimal extensions which specify a fixed order of subdivisions under a single class number are called successive cutter numbers. Successive cutter numbers are "used to designate a subject subclass, indicate the form of material, or signal further geographical subarrangement."[1]

Several different modes have been used to present successive cutter numbers. The current model is easily recognized by its form. Some of the variations are not quite so obvious. The current form is displayed in the first four examples. Examples 5 through 8 feature the variations. Where regions or countries are called for by captions, preassigned cutter numbers may be taken from the Table of Regions and Countries in One Alphabet.

CURRENT NOTATION

The current notational structure of successive cutter numbers consists of the following:

1. a directional "Under each" statement in which the source of the cutter number is usually named, followed by the successive subarrangement consisting of
2. a lower-case x preceded by a decimal representing the first subdivision of the subject, and
3. for each succeeding subdivision, a lower-case x preceded by a decimal plus a digit or digits.

The selected cutter number replaces the x in the class number and, once chosen, remains constant throughout the succession. The digit following each .x becomes a part of the class number as it denotes the succession of the particular subdivision in a call number.

EXAMPLE 1

```
                        City planning
                          Zoning
                            By region or country
HT169.8                       Other regions or countries, A-Z
                              Under each country:
                                .x      General works
                                .x2     Local, A-Z
```

OBSERVE

1. A single class number is assigned to Other regions or countries.

2. The successive cutter numbers are introduced by Under each country.

3. Cutter numbers are to be taken from the names of countries.

4. There are two subdivisions for each country.

5. The .x for the first subdivision is not followed by a digit.

6. The digit 2 follows the second .x to indicate treatment of the subject in a particular locality of the country represented by the cutter number.

7. The A-Z after Local means that a second cutter number representing a specific local area of the country is to be the third element of a call number.

EXAMPLE 2

```
                    Trade unions.  Labor unions.  Workingmen's associations
                       History
                         Medieval (to 1789).  Guilds
                           By region or country
HD6473                       Other regions or countries, A-Z
                             Under each country:
                               .xA1-3        Periodicals.  Societies.  Serials
                               .xA6-Z        General works
                                             By period
                               .x2A3-39       Origins.  Earliest history
                               .x2A6-Z        Later (16th-18th century)
                               .x3A-Z        By industry or trade, A-Z
                               .x4A-Z        Local, A-Z
```

OBSERVE

1. The x is to be replaced by the cutter numbers for countries other than those printed in the schedule before Other regions or countries.

2. There are several subdivisions.

3. Successive cutter numbers and dedicated cutter numbers are combined in the sequence.

EXAMPLE 2, continued

4. There is only one class number.

5. Second cutter numbers are provided for .x3 and .x4 by A-Z after the subdivision.

6. For .x3, second cutter numbers are to be assigned from the names of industries and trades; for .x4 from the names of localities of a country.

EXAMPLE 3

Shipping
   Interior navigation
      By region or country
         United States

HE633   By company, A-Z
            Under each company, A-Z
        .x   Charter, etc.
        .x2 Regular reports
        .x3 Special reports
        .x4 Registers
        .x5 Other

OBSERVE

1. The table applies to the United States only.

2. There are several successive cutter numbers.

3. The cutter numbers for companies in the United States replace the x.

4. The digits after x represent various forms of publications issued by companies.

PROCEDURE

The general procedure for applying successive cutter numbers is given below; then Example 3 is worked out.

1. Determine the appropriate cutter number for the work as designated by the subdivision.

2. Substitute the cutter number for x to form the class number for the first topic in the Under each statement.

3. Substitute the cutter number for the x before each Arabic numeral to form the class numbers for each of the other subdivisions in the Under each statement.

According to the caption for HE633 In Example 3, x equals the names of shipping companies in the United States. One such company, the Fall River Line whose cutter number was found in the <u>Library of Congress Shelflist</u>, is used in the illustrative procedural steps.

Step I
The cutter number for the Fall River Line is F3.

Step 2
Substituting F3 for x in the Under each statement results in HE633.F3 for the company's charters.

Step 3
Substituting F3 before the other successive digits yields these class numbers for the other subdivisions:

HE633	HE633	HE633	HE633
.F32	.F33	.F34	.F35

Further subdivision is not indicated after any of the subdivisions in Example 3. Cutter numbers taken from main entries would complete the call numbers.

When the fourth edition of Class H was published, there were several internal tables with a cutter-number column. Subsequently, the columns were cancelled from the tables for HE2810-3560 (Railways) and HE4501-5260 (Street railways. Subways. Rapid transit systems). Example 4 is one of the few remaining internal tables containing a cutter-number column.

EXAMPLE 4

Traffic engineering. Roads and highways. Streets
  History
    Medieval and modern

HE353   General works
      By region or country
       Under each country (unless otherwise provided for):

I no.	Cutter no.	
.A1-3	.x	Periodicals. Serials
.A4-Z54	.x2	General works
.Z55A-Z	.x3	Special topics, A-Z
		For list of topics, <u>see</u> HE336
.Z6A-Z	.x4	By region or province, A-$\overline{Z}$
		Including special roads
.Z7A-Z	.x5	By city, A-Z

United States
355.A3A1-29   Periodicals. Serials
    .A5-Z   General works
    .3   Special topics
        For list of topics, <u>see</u> HE336; for special topics
         applicable to special places, <u>see</u> HE356+
    356   By region or state, A-Z
        Including interstate roads, e.g. .C4, Capital Beltway;
         .C8, Cumberland Road; .L4, Lee Highway; .L7
        Lincoln Highway

	For Intrastate roads, <u>see</u> the state, e.g., .N5,
	Garden State Parkway, New Jersey
.5	By city, A-Z
357	Canada
	Other American regions or countries
	Including Latin America (General)
358	General works
359	By region or country, A-Z
	Europe
361	General works
363	By region or country, A-Z
365	Asia. By region or country, A-Z
	Africa
366.5	General works
367	By region or country, A-Z
368	Australia
.2	New Zealand
.5	Pacific Islands, A-Z
	Hawaii, <u>see</u> HE356.H3

<u>OBSERVE</u>

Under the heading Cutter no., successive cutter numbers indicate subdivisions in the Internal table.

The United States has all of its subdivisions printed in the schedule and, therefore, is exempted from the internal table's provisions. The question, then, is which range column to use with other geographical units? The subdivision By region or country, A-Z, accompanying a geographical area signals the assignment of successive cutter numbers. Guide cards in the <u>Library of Congress Shelflist</u> confirmed use of the numbers.

	HE363 EUROPE		HE 367 AFRICA	
	Denmark	Finland	Cameroon	Egypt
Documents	.D4	.F5	.C35	.E29
General works	.D42	.F52	.C352	.E3
Special subjects	.D43	.F53	.C353	.E32
By province or region, A-Z	.D44	.F45	.C354	.E33
By city, A-Z	.D45	.F55	.C355	.E34

Note that there are some differences in the wording of the subdivisions on the guide cards and those in the internal table from the fourth edition of Class H. A later revision of the table adds Societies to the first subdivision.

Call numbers on catalog entries in the <u>Library of Congress Shelflist</u> confirmed use of the one-number range column.

	Canada	Australia
General works	HE357	HE368
	.B78	.P35
By region or province, A-Z	HE357	HE368
	.Z6S26	.Z6W47
	(Saskatchewan)	(Western Australia)
By city, A-Z	HE357	HE368
	.Z6M6	.Z7B77
	(Montreal)	(Brisbane)

For General works, book numbers complete the call number. For By region or province and By city, a cutter number for the appropriate geographical area assigned after the dedicated cutter number completes the call number.

The current form of successive cutter number indication serves in internal tables as subarrangements under subdivisions. An example is the subarrangement under By industry or trade, A-Z, In the table for HD6521-6940.5 (Trade unions. Labor unions. Workingmen's associations).

VARIATIONS

At variance are: 1. the placement of the notice of successive cutter numbers in their current style; 2. the provision of topical cutter numbers to be applied successively; and 3. the announcement of succession by means other than the use of x. Variations one and two are illustrated in Examples 5 and 6 in different ways. Variation three is shown in Examples 7 and 8 in different ways. For Example 5, a short section of the "Ts" has been excerpted from the lengthy alphabetical list of industries and trades under the class number HD8039 (Labor).

EXAMPLE 5

	Labor	
HD8039	By industry or trade, A-Z[1]	
	.T16	Taxicab drivers
	.T2	Teamsters
	.T24	Telecommunication workers
		Telegraphers

EXAMPLE 5, continued
_____

.T25   Commercial
.T27   Railroad
.T3   Telephone workers

_____
1.   For subarrangement under each, see footnote, p. 88 IN H-HJ.

OBSERVE

1.   HD8039 is the sole class number for the entire list of industries and trades.
2.   Topical cutter numbers are printed in the schedule.
3.   It is not obvious that the printed cutter numbers are to be treated successively.
4.   Subarrangement directions have been placed in a footnote.

_____

That the suggested cutter numbers in Example 5 are to be handled successively is revealed in the footnote on the first page of HD8039. The footnote reads: "Under each: subarrange as follows: .x General works, .x2 By region or country, A-Z, e.g., .C3, Carpenters; .C32U6, Carpenters in the United States." The term successive cutter numbers is not used. The class numbers for Telecommunications workers would be

HD8039   HD8039
.T24   .T242

Example 6 shows a partial list of one group of products extracted from HD9000-9999 (Special industries and trades). The extract is typical of the organizational scheme for the special products, industries and trades.

EXAMPLE 6
_____

Agricultural and other plant and animal products.
Food products
HD9240-9259   Fruits and nuts
    9259   Special products, A-Z
        .A45-47   Almonds
        .A5-6   Apples
        .A95-954   Avocados
        .B2-3   Bananas
        .B46-464   Betel nuts

EXAMPLE 6, continued _____

.B52-524	Blueberries
.B7-74	Brazil nuts
.C3-33	Cashew nuts

1. For subarrangement, see tables, pp. 122-124 in H-HJ.

OBSERVE

1. HD9240-9259, representing fruits and nuts, is a range of twenty numbers.
2. The special products are assigned one class number, the last number in the range.
3. Each special product is allocated a spread of cutter numbers based on the product's initial letter.
4. Notice of subarrangement has been relegated to a footnote.
5. The footnote does not disclose how the cutter spans are to be applied, referring instead to tables located elsewhere.

_____

On the pages cited in the footnote are Tables of Subdivisions under Industries and Trades (HD9000-9999), A, B, C, D. Table A (20 nos.), is appropriate for fruits and nuts. Sequential number 19, Special products, A-Z, corresponds to HD9259. The instruction for special products states that successive cutter numbers are to be used. Subdivisions are then assigned to four, three, and two cutter-number spans in the .x style. Observe the application of the successive cutter numbers displayed in Example 6:

1. Apples--a two-cutter number product.

   .x   General works. History.
              Including biography
   .x2   Local, A-Z
              HD9259   HD9259
              .A5   .A6

2. Cashew nuts--a three-cutter number product.

   .x   Periodicals. Societies. Serials
   .x2   General works. History
              Including biography
   .x3   Local, A-Z
              HD9259   HD9259   HD9259
              .C3   .C32   .C33

3.   Brazil nuts--a four-cutter number product.

    .x   Periodicals. Societies. Serials
    .x2   General works. History
             Including biography
    .x3   Local, A-Z
    .x4   Firms, A-Z

HD9259	HD9259	HD9259	HD9259
.B7	.B72	.B73	.B74

A note accompanying Special products, Tables A and B, issues some further directions for subarrangement to be applied where needed. Added is the cautionary word that "one" is generally omitted as a final cutter-number digit.

Occasionally, a Subarranged like note at the point of application specifies the appropriate table and sequential number to be used. The note appears in the following manner:

                    Mineral and metal industries
HD9539.A4-Z   Particular metals, A-Z
                    Subarrange each like Table A(19), B(10), p. 124

The next two examples show two other methods by which successive cuttering is made known. Although obsolete, the method in Example 8 can still be encountered in Class H.

EXAMPLE 7

                    Direct taxes (Special)
                 Income tax
                  By region or country
                   United States
                    States
HJ4655.A1   States collectively
  .A2-W   Individual states, A-W

                      For subdivisions under the several states, use successive Cutter numbers; use a single digit for "General works," two digits for the preceding and following subdivisions.

                    e.g.   Michigan
                      .M47   Periodicals. Societies. Serials
                      .M5   General works
                                Special
                      .M52   Capital income
                      .M53   Foreign income
                      .M54   Other
                      .M55   Administration

OBSERVE

1.   A note beneath the class number states explicitly that successive cutter numbers are to be used.

37

2. The note also describes how to apply the digits successively but without x as a symbol.

3. As a pattern, successive cutter numbers applied to one state are shown.

Inserts in the Library of Congress Shelflist for HJ4655 furnished spans of numbers for the following states:

California	.C16-24	Oregon	.O65-72
Colorado	.C66-74	Pennsylvania	.P45-458
Iowa	.I76-84	Tennessee	.T216-224
New York	.N46-55	Wisconsin	.W55-65

EXAMPLE 8

```
                    Handicapped
                     Deaf
                      By region or country
                       United States
HV2561                  By region or state, A-Z
                         Under each state:
                          (1) General works
                          (2) State institutions
                          (3) Other institutions, By city, A-Z
```

OBSERVE

1. A single class number is assigned to By region or state.

2. An Under each statement introduces the subdivisions.

3. The subdivisions are represented by parenthesized Arabic numbers.

The parenthesized Arabic numbers in Example 8 can easily be mistaken for sequential numbering in a one-number range column of an internal table. The presentation diverges from standard internal table provisions in two ways. First, sequential numbering normally agrees with class numbers. There are three sequential numbers but only one class number. Second, dedicated cutter numbers customarily represent subdivisions in one-number range columns. Arabic numbers in the single column denote the succession of subdivisions in the call number.

That the Arabic numbers indicate succession was verified in the Library of Congress Shelflist. Two guide cards filed for HV2561 gave the numbers for Tennessee and Virginia.

Tennessee T3-33		Virginia V8-83
.T3A-Z	General works	.V8A-Z
.T32A-Z	State institutions	.V82A-Z
.T33	Other institutions,	.V83
	By city, A-Z	

Mary Arick describes the application of the parenthesized numbers under the heading "Double Cuttering."[2] Although the term successive cutter numbers is not used, the example demonstrates that the digits are applied successively.

NOTES

1. Martha L. Manheimer, Cataloging and Classification: A Workbook, 2nd ed. rev. and exp. (New York: Dekker, 1980), p. 81.

2. Mary C. Arick, "Subclassification and Book Numbers of Documents and Official Publications," in The Use of the Library of Congress Classification; Proceedings of the Institute on the Use of the Library of Congress Classification, ed. by Richard H. Schimmelpfeng and C. Donald Cook (Chicago; American Library Association, 1968), pp. 148-149.

chapter 5
internal tables

In Class H, detailed subdivisions of subjects are frequently presented in internal tables, so-called because they are printed within the schedule (in contrast to the geographical tables which are printed at the end of the schedule). Internal tables prescribe the sequence or pattern of subdivisions to be applied within given spans of class numbers. As with "Subarranged like," internal tables obviate the necessity for repeating common subdivisions.

As each table is designed to fit a particular subject, the tables vary widely in their content, their order, and their extent. Some of these variations can be seen in the examples selected for this chapter. The important point to remember is that the tables and number spans make up a partnership and, therefore, neither is to be used alone.

Normally, internal tables are introduced by an Under each statement which usually names the element from which cutter numbers are to be taken; usually the tables are unnumbered. There are some exceptions to the latter: 1. three tables between HJ3360-3361.9 and HJ3370-3374 have been given Arabic numbers; 2. two tables for subdividing HS1510 have been assigned Roman numbers; and 3. the four Tables of Subdivisions Under Industries and Trades, HD9000-9999, have been labelled A, B, C, D.

The tables are presented either immediately before a classified list of geographical divisions--each place accompanied by assigned class numbers--or immediately following a range of class numbers and the geographical caption. If the latter, one of the Tables of Geographical Divisions will be cited after the caption. The places will be found in the central column of the Tables.

Internal tables are composed of two main elements:

1. Subdivisions

   On the right is a list of subdivisions for the subject. Subdivisions may be topical, geographical, historical, type of material, or any combination of these.

2. Range columns

a. On the left are one or more columns headed by the range of numbers assigned to geographical divisions in the schedule or in the Tables of Geographical Divisions -- 10 nos., 5 nos., etc. Countries are referred to by the extent of their range numbers: ten-number countries, five-number countries.

b. The columns are arranged according to the headings in descending numerical order from left to right, ending with a cutter-number column, if there is one.

c. Beneath each heading is a sequence of Arabic numbers, successive cutter numbers, or dedicated cutter numbers corresponding to the numbers in the heading and to the subdivisions. The sequential numbers under the headings indicate which number within a given place-number range matches a particular subdivision. In columns headed 20 nos. through 2 nos., sequential indication is expressed by ordinary numbers enclosed in parentheses. In columns headed 1 no., dedicated cutter numbers routinely replace the Arabic numbers. Cutter-number columns show standard successive cutter-number indicators. Occasionally, part of the sequential indication is given other than in range columns. Directions for one-number and two-number countries have been placed in a note at the end of the internal table for HJ4661-4752 (Income tax).

In addition to representing subdivisions in one-number columns, dedicated cutter numbers also represent subdivisions in other range columns as extensions of sequential numbers. The internal table for Other regions and countries before HJ6750-6757 (Customs administration) shows dedicated cutter numbers in each of its five range columns.

Successive cutter numbers are presented in internal tables as subarrangements under subdivisions as well as in cutter number columns. In the internal table for HD8101-8942.5 (Labor), the subdivisions By region or country, A-Z, and By city, A-Z, have successive cutter-number subarrangements.

The examples illustrate the main features and characteristics of internal tables. The selected tables apply to classified listings of geographical areas in the schedule. The application of internal tables associated with the Tables of Geographical Divisions is described in Chapter 7, Geographical Order.

EXAMPLE I

Statistical data
  For data of special fields, <u>see</u> the field
Universal statistics
HA154	Periodicals. Societies. Serials
155	General works

EXAMPLE 1, continued

By region or country
Class here general statistics and censuses, including
population and vital statistics if consisting of the
broadest groups of data. For population and vital
statistics limited to a more specific subject. <u>see</u>
HB884+, e.g. HB1321, Mortality
Under each country (unless otherwise provided for):

20 nos.	10 nos.	5 nos.	1 no.	
				Official
(1)	(1)	(1)	.A1-3	Main serial
(2)				Statistical abstracts
(3)				Other serials
(4)	(1.5)	(1.5)	.A4-5	Censuses. By date
(5)	(2)	(2)		Other monographic works
				Administrative reports of the
				census and other statistical
				bureaus, <u>see</u> HA37+
(9)	(3)			Miscellaneous
		(3)		Nonofficial
(14)	(5)		.A6-Z	Serials
(15)	(6)			General works
(16)				Manuals
(17)				Miscellaneous
(18)	(7)	(4)	.Z9A-Z	By state, etc., A-Z
(19)	(8)	(5)		By city, A-Z
		America		
175		General works		
195-730		United States		
		Official		
		Serials, <u>see</u> HA203		
195		General works		

Class here works summarizing the results of
more than one census period

OBSERVE

1. An Under each country statement introduces the internal table.
2. The table precedes the locations. Each has been given a number span in the schedule. The United States is partially exempt from the table because some of its subdivisions have been assigned individual class numbers in the schedule.
3. Different number ranges are allocated to the places as shown by the column headings 20 nos., 10 nos., etc.
4. Columns headed 20 nos. and 10 nos. have some unassigned sequential numbers.
5. Decimal extensions of sequential numbers appear in the 10 nos. and 5 nos. columns.
6. Some subdivisions lack sequential numbering in the range columns.
7. An A and Z dedicated cutter number sequence is supplied for one-number countries.

Several changes have been made to the internal table in Example I. Among the changes are the deletion of Official, Nonofficial, and Miscellaneous subdivisions and the assignment of 201 as the first class number for the United States.

PROCEDURE

The general technique for forming class numbers when applying internal tables is essentially one of matching country range numbers to the sequential numbers in the table. A class number obtained by the following steps would represent the subject, the place, and a subdivision of the subject.

1. Determine the number range of the area in question; e.g., 1 no., 4 nos., etc.
2. Match the range to the appropriate range column in the internal table.
3. Find the specific subdivision in the right-hand column which is treated in the work being classified.
4. Match the subdivision with the Arabic number, dedicated or successive cutter number opposite the subdivision in the appropriate range column. If a subdivision lacks a sequential number opposite it, use the numbering in the range column for the preceding subdivision.
5. Select the number from the country's number range which corresponds to the sequential indication in no. 4.
6. Attach cutter numbers as required.

To illustrate these steps, Brazil has been chosen from Example I. The work to be classified concerns statistical data for Brasilia, the capital city.

Step 1

In the schedule following the table, Brazil has been allotted the span 971-990 making it a twenty-number country.

Step 2

The 20 nos. column in the table matches Brazil's span.

Steps 3 and 4

The applicable subdivision is By city which corresponds to (19) in the 20 nos. column.

Step 5

The nineteenth number in Brazil's number range is 989.

Step 6

Cutter on the city's name as indicated by A-Z: B7 Brasilia. Attach a main-entry cutter number.

The class number then would be HA989.B7 to which a main entry cutter would be added to form the complete call number. If a work on the same subject was being classified for a one-number country, .Z9 would be inserted before the city cutter number. For Finland, a one-number country whose capital is Helsinki, the call number would be HA1450.5.Z9H4. Note that a state of a one-number country would also be assigned .Z9.

EXAMPLE 2

Public finance
History and conditions
By region or country
Europe
Subarrangement for HJ1190-1294 (Unless otherwise provided for):

10 nos.	5 nos.		1 no.	
((1)	(0) or (5)		.A1-Z5	General works
				History
(2)	(1)	(6).A3		Through 1789
(3)		.A6-Z		1790-1900
(4)	(2)	(7)		20th century
	(3)	(8)		Organization and administration
(6)			.Z6	General works
(7)				Early
(8)				Special
(9)	(4)	(9)		States, provinces
.A1A-Z	.A1A-Z	.A1A-Z	.Z7A-Z	Collective
				Including grants-in-aid
.A2-Z	.A2-Z	.A2-Z	.Z8A-Z	Individual

HJ1190-1193	Benelux countries. Low Countries.
1195-1199	Belgium
1200-1204	Netherlands
1204.5	Luxemburg
	Soviet Union
1205	General works
	History
1206	1801-1900
1207	1901-1917
1208	1917-
	Organization and administration
1210	General works
1211	Special
.5	Local, A-Z
1212	Finland
1213	Poland
1215-1218	Scandinavia
1220-1224	Denmark
1225-1229	Iceland
1230-1234	Norway
1235-1239	Sweden
1240-1249	Spain
1250-1254	Portugal
1255-1264	Switzerland
	Cantons
1264.A2	Collective
.A5-Z	Individual

EXAMPLE 2, continued
_____

	Balkan States
.5	Albania
1265-1269	Bulgaria
1275-1279	Romania
1290-1294	Yugoslavia

OBSERVE

1. The internal table precedes the geographical areas, each with assigned class numbers.

2. For 5 nos., there are two columns of sequential numbers with five numbers each.

3. One column begins with zero; the other with five.

4. Belgium and Netherland's number spans consist of five numbers each.

5. The table applies only to countries assigned class numbers within the range span HJ1190-1294.

_____

The procedure for applying a five-number double range column is still that of matching range numbers and sequential numbers. Match country number ranges whose first numbers end in zero with the column headed (0). Match country number ranges whose first numbers end in five with the column headed (5). Without attaching the dedicated cutter numbers, the class numbers for Belgium and Netherlands in Example 3 would be:

HJ1195	HJ1200
HJ1196	HJ1201
HJ1197	HJ1202
HJ1198	HJ1203
HJ1199	HJ1204

Even though Benelux countries and Scandinavia in Example 3 have only four numbers, the 5 nos. column can be applied to them simply by omitting (4) and (9). These two sequential numbers are for local areas. Local units of the two regions are the named countries beneath them in the schedule.

A slightly different double-column internal table precedes HG9969.5 (Other insurance). The table numbers are decimals and are without parentheses. The absence of parentheses indicates that the numbers are not sequential. Rather, the numbers themselves are to be attached to the class numbers for the several kinds of insurance listed. The subdivision Policies in the table has the number .23 for class numbers ending in zero and .63 for class numbers ending in five. Automobile insurance policies would be HG9970.23; burglary insurance policies, HG975.63.

Example 3 is somewhat different from the internal tables of Examples 1 and 2. There is a single column of ordinal numbers for subdivisions in the table.

	Local finance
	By region or country
	Other regions or countries
	Europe
HJ9415	General works
9420	European Economic Community countries
	Great Britain
9421	General works
	History. By period
9422.A3	Through 1700
.A4	18th century
.A5	1800-1860
.A6-Z	1861-1900
9423	1901-
9424	National supervision and control.
	"Grants in aid," etc.
	Other special
	Under each:

	(1)	General works
		History. By period
	.A3A-Z	Early works through 1800
	.A5A-Z	1801-1860
	(2)	1861-1900
	(3)	1901-
	(4)	Special, A-Z
9425-9428	Taxation. Revenue
9429-9432	Credit. Debt. Loans
9433-9436	Administration
9438	Cities, towns, A-Z
	Subarranged like HJ9193

OBSERVE

1.   The single-column internal table under Other special applies to one country.

2.   Four sequential numbers are provided in the table.

3.   Four additional subdivisions are provided with four-number range spans to match the four sequential numbers in the table.

The Subarranged like note for HJ9438 in Example 3 can be disregarded. Library of Congress has cancelled the note.

Now and then, the parenthetical phrase "Unless otherwise provided for" is a part of the table directions. The phrase means that the pattern of the internal table does not apply to every place listed. Allowance is made thus for those countries whose development varies from the table pattern. To discover the exceptions, examine the list of geographical areas noting those whose subdivisions are set forth by schedule notation. In the list of countries for HJ2775-2889

(Public finance), the subdivisions for the Soviet Union and Switzerland are printed in the schedule. Historical subdivisions and local units differ from those of the internal table.

Quite frequently, with or without notice, subdivisions for the United States are set apart in the schedule from other countries. Actually, the majority of internal tables serve other regions and countries. Notice of exclusion of the United States from internal table provisions may be given by the phrase (Except the United States), in parentheses after the Under each statement. The exception is illustrated in the table instructions for HV741-803 (Protection, assistance and relief for children). In the same way, the District of Columbia has been excluded from the provisions in the internal table before HJ9191-9193 (Local finance. States) and given dedicated cutter numbers in the alphabetical state list.

The class numbers HJ8101-HJ8898 for the geographical division of Public credit illustrate the employment of various internal tables for different territorial divisions under the same subject. First, the United States is given detailed development by class numbers in the schedule including a table for regions and a table for states individually. Then, instead of one table for all the other areas, as is often true, there are separate tables for Central America, South America, Europe, Balkan states, and finally, an internal table for the remaining countries and a citation to a Table of Geographical Divisions.

chapter 6
general special

Perhaps "General works" and "General works, treatises, and textbooks" need little explanation, if any, but the subdivisions "General special" and "General special (special aspects of the subject as a whole)" as subject devices enumerated in the schedule are likely to be a bit troublesome. Here are three expressions of the meaning of General special.

> The provision for "General" or "General works" often appears in sequence with the provision for "General special," which means special aspects relating to the subject as a whole and does not include any hierarchial divisions or branches of the subject. In some of the recent editions of L.C. schedules, the caption "Special aspects of the subject as a whole" accompanies, or appears in place of, the caption "General special."[1]

> ...the use of a number and the term "General special" to provide, not only for the general subject in a special situation, but also for a new aspect of a subject until that aspect is recognized by a distinctive number.[2]

> ... "General special" is used for works on the general subject but dealing with it from a particular point of view or with respect to a particular relationship. For example, in the Class HF (Commerce) schedule, "Treatises" on advertising [HF5821+] are followed by "General special" for works on advertising in foreign countries [HF5827]. In HE (Transportation and Communication), general works on transportation [HE151] precede "General special" [HE152.5] for those dealing with transportation from the point of view of public policy and state ownership. Another example can be found in Class HB (Economics), where general works on crises and business cycles [HB3711] are followed by "General special" for such topics as costs and profits and crises, consumption and crises, social aspects of crises, etc. [HB3718-3728.5].[3]

Wherever divisions are captioned "General special" or "General special (special aspects of the subject as a whole)," they follow "General works," although there can be intervening topics. That order is both logical and invariable. The examples in the third quotation and those which follow present some of the kinds of topics encompassed by General special. Examples 1 and 2 are accompanied by abbreviated catalog entries from The Library of Congress Shelflist. Subject headings convey the General special aspects treated in those cataloged works. Cutter numbers were assigned from main entries.

EXAMPLE I

	Automotive transportation
HE5611	General works
5613	General special

OBSERVE

1. General works precede General special.
2. Topics to be included in General special are not indicated.

HE5613	L'Automobile dans la socíeté [Par] A[lbert]
.A92	Godart

      I. Automobiles - Social aspects.

HE5613	Cooke, Peter Nicholas Collins.
.C66	The company car: its allocation,
1973	Acquisition, and administration.

      I. Automobiles, Company.

HE5613	National Computing Centre Limited.
.N35	Computers in vehicle scheduling.

      I. Electronic data processing –

Transportation, Automotive - Dispatching.

HE5613	National Research Council. Highway Research
.N37	Board.

Motorist aid systems.

      I. Transportation, Automotive.

  2. Traffic Safety.

EXAMPLE 2

	Sociology
	General works, treatises, and advanced textbooks
HM51	English
55	French
57	German
59	Italian
61	Other European languages
62	Oriental languages, A-Z
63	Other languages, A-Z

	Elementary textbooks
66	General works
68	Syllabi, outlines
73	General special

OBSERVE

1. Although General works precedes General special, General special does not immediately follow General works.

2. Special aspects to be included in HM73 are not indicated.

HM73
.C37

Cartwright, Dorwin, ed.

Studies in social power.

I. Power (Social sciences) - Collections.

HM73
.N37

Narr, Wolf Dicter.

Pluralistische Gesellschaft.

I. Pluralism (Social sciences). 2. Democracy.

HM73
.N45

Nelson, Jack L.

Introduction to value inquiry.

I. Social values. 2. Decision making.

HM73
.S358

Schwartz, Barry.

Queuing and waiting: studies in the social organization of access and delay.

I. Time allocation. 2. Queuing theory. 3. Social Interaction.

HM73

Schwendter, Rolf.

Theorie der Subkultur.

I. Subculture .

HM73
.S38

Scott, John Paul.

Social control and social change.

I. Social control - Addresses, essays, lectures.

EXAMPLE 3

	Public finance
	History and conditions
	By region or country
	Europe
	France
HJ1071	General works
1072	General special
	e.g. Caisse des dépôts et consignations

OBSERVE

One general special aspect is quoted.

Two additional points in regard to the General special category to be noted are that
General special may be defined by alphabetically arranged lists in the schedule and that the
special aspects may not be captioned with either of the standard phrases. Example 4 illustrates
those points.

EXAMPLE 4

	Socialism. Communism. Anarchism
	General works - Continued
HX518	Special topics, A-Z
	.C7 Self-criticism
	.L4 Leadership
	.R4 Revisionism
	Self-criticism, see .C7
	.S8 Strategy
519	Communism/socialism and cooperation
	Cf. HD2951+, Economic history
520	Communism/socialism and architecture
521	Communism/socialism and art
522	Communism/socialism and creative ability
523	Communism/socialism and culture
526	Communism/socialism and education
	Cf. HX19, Study and teaching of socialism
	Communism/socialism and ethics, see BJ1388+
528	Communism/socialism and intellectuals
530	Communism/socialism and the law
531	Communism/socialism and literature
	Cf. PN56.S66, Socialist realism in literature
533	Communism/socialism and philosophy
535	Communism/socialism and psychology
536	Communism/socialism and religion
541	Communism/socialism and science
.5	Communism/socialism and social sciences

542		Communism/socialism and society
544		Communism/socialism and trade unions
545		Communism/socialism and war
546		Communism/socialism and woman. Communism/socialism and the family
547		Communism/socialism and youth
550		Communism/socialism in relation to other topics, A-Z
	.A56	Anthropology
	.A7	Armies
	.B8	Buddhism
	.E25	Ecology
	.F47	Finance
	.F7	Freemasons
	.G45	Geography
	.I5	International relations
	.I8	Islam
	.J4	Jews. Judaism
	.L3	Land question
	.L55	Linguistics
	.L7	Liquor problem
	.M35	Mass media
	.M4	Medicine
	.M6	Middle classes
	.M65	Motion pictures
	.N3	Nationalism
	.N66	Nonviolence
	.P4	Peasantry
	.P7	Property
	.P77	Psychoanalysis
	.T7	Trusts

OBSERVE

1. The General special aspects, HX519-547, follow General works.

2. The special aspects are not captioned by either standard phrase.

3. Under HX550, topical cutter numbers are assigned to the special aspects.

For further guidance, some additional subject headings for General special and General special (Special aspects of the subject as a whole) are presented. The headings were taken from Library of Congress Shelflist catalog entries under the General special class numbers which follow the subjects.

Women. Feminism. HQ1233
  Women in public life
  Women in politics

Organization of production. Management. Industrial
    management. HD38
  Organizational change
  Creative ability in business
  Comparative management
  Diversification in industry
  Management by objectives
  Decentralization in management
  Management - Psychological aspects

Accounting. Bookkeeping. HF5657
  Accounting - Social aspects
  Disclosure in accounting
  Inflation (Finance) and accounting
  Accounting - Computer programs
  Current value accounting

Labor market. Labor supply and demand. HD5707
  Employment forecasting
  Employment stabilization
  Labor mobility
  Labor turnover
  Labor supply - Mathematical models

General special is also presented as a subdivision in internal tables. The table for HD5501-5630.7 (Arbitration and conciliation) contains an example.

NOTES

1. Lois M. Chan, Immroth's Guide to the Library of Congress Classification, 3rd ed. (Littleton, Colo.: Libraries Unlimited, 1980), p. 50.

2. Mary D. Herrick, "Orientation of Staff and Clientele into the Library of Congress Classification," in The Use of the Library of Congress Classification; Proceedings of the Institute on the Use of the Library of Congress Classification, ed. by Richard H. Schimmelpfeng and C. Donald Cook (Chicago: American Library Association, 1968), p. 187.

3. Charles C. Bead, "The Library of Congress Classification: Development, Characteristics, and Structure," in The Use of the Library of Congress Classification; Proceedings of the Institute on the Use of the Library of Congress Classification, ed. by Richard H. Schimmelpfeng and C. Donald Cook (Chicago: American Library Association, 1968), p. 25.

chapter 7
geographical order

This chapter takes its charge from Nicholas Hedlesky:

...it will be most useful to devote major attention to the use of the principal tables with which Class H is provided, <u>in particular to the means by which the literature of a class is subdivided: by country and within each country, by category and topic.</u>[1] (italics added)

"By country," or geographical order, qualifies for "major attention" in Class H because most social science subjects as outlined in the Class are applicable to the territorial divisions of the world.   In Class H, subdivision by geographical area is the most common form of detailed enumeration.[2]

Basically, there are two principles of geographical organization: alphabetical and classified. They are sometimes combined under the same subject. Leo LaMontagne states that both the order and extent of geographical subdivisions are adapted to the subject under which they apply.[3] An examination of the "means" of subdividing social science subjects geographically follows.

GEOGRAPHICAL AUTHORIZATION

Captions authorizing geographical subdivision name the kinds of areas to be included. Commonly used phrases are:

1. By region or country -- the general overall authorization phrase meaning the regions and countries of the world. It almost invariably introduces geographical subdivision.
2. Other regions and countries -- the cover phrase for those areas not treated beforehand in the schedule under the general direction. It oft-times signals a change of subarrangement: to another internal table, alphabetical order, etc. The word "Other" may be used in combinations such as Other divisions of Asia, A-Z. Note that "By" does not precede the instruction.

3. By region or state
4. By region or province
5. By province
6. By island
7. By State
8. By city

To these phrases may be added By country, By place, and Local. By country, an absolete phrase, is to be understood to mean By region or country, unless contrary instructions are given.[4] By place occurs infrequently as it is being phased out. "By" does not precede Local. Other area divisional words--regions, cities, etc.--also occur without the aid of the preposition.

The geographical directions all name land divisions; however, By region or country includes water areas when appropriate. HE597 (Shipping. Traffic. Freight. By region or country, A-Z) is accompanied by the example .B3 Baltic Sea.

It is essential to understand the use of base numbers in geographical subdivision. The numbers have significance for both alphabetical and classified subplans.

BASE NUMBERS

When Table of States II and III or one of the Tables of Geographical Divisions is to be used in the construction of a class number, the table number is designated after the class-number range and geographical direction. The Tables are located at the end of the schedule. Following the table number, there is a superscript to a footnote. The footnote instructs the user to add the state or country number from the table to a number in the footnote. That number is called the base number. It usually ends in zero and is one less than the first number in the number range assigned in front of the caption.

PROCEDURE

The procedure for applying a base number consists of two main steps:

1. obtain the state or country number from the appropriate Table; and
2. add the base number to the state or country number.

The total of the two numbers should fall within the assigned class-number range. If there is an internal table, the appropriate sequential indication must be selected. The steps are illustrated following Examples 1 and 2. Both employ a Table of Geographical Divisions. Further details for combining an internal table with a Table of Geographical Divisions are outlined in the section of this chapter on the Tables. Examples of the procedure for Table of States II and III will be found in Chapter 10, States. The steps are the same.

EXAMPLE I

Business cycles. Economic fluctuations.
HB3741-3840   By region or country. Table I[1]

I. For Table I, see pp. 331-340 in H-HJ. Add country number in table to 3740.

OBSERVE

I. The range of class numbers precedes the geographical authorization.

2. Table I of the Tables of Geographical Divisions is cited. (There is only one number per country in Table I).

3. The base number in the footnote is one less than the first range number.

Africa is used to illustrate the steps for applying the base number in Example I.

$$\begin{array}{ll} 3740 & \text{The base number in the footnote} \\ +\ 82 & \text{The number for Africa in Table I} \\ \hline \text{HB3822} & \text{The class number for the subject in Africa} \end{array}$$

Note that the sum of the two numbers is within the confines of the class number range.

EXAMPLE 2

Labor
Social insurance. Social security. Pensions.
HD7121-7250.7   By region or country. Table V[1]
Under each country:

4 nos.	I no.	
(I)	.A1-5	Periodicals
(3)	.A7-Z7	General works
(4)	.Z8A-Z	Local, A-Z

I. For Table V see pp. 331-340 in H-HJ. Add country number in table to 7120.

OBSERVE

I. A Table of Geographical Divisions is quoted.

2. Subdivisions are presented in an internal table.

3. According to the internal table, some countries will have one number and some four numbers in Table V.

Colombia is a one-number country in Table V. Add the base number as follows:

7120	The base number in the footnote
+ 37	The number for Colombia in Table V
HD7157	The class number for the subject in Colombia

HD7157 falls within the range of numbers assigned to the regions and countries. Applying the 1 no. column of the internal table, two calls numbers could be:

HD7157	A periodical on the subject beginning with
.35	Boletin

HD7157	A work on the subject in Bogata, Colombia
.Z8B6	

India has the range 97-100 in Table V making it a four-number country. Those numbers are added to the base number to represent the subdivisions in the internal table.

7120	7120	7120	The base number in the footnote
+97	+ 99	+100	The numbers for India in Table V
HD7217	HD7219	HD7220	The class numbers for the three subdivisions in the table on the subject in India

Under 4 nos. in the internal table, sequential number (2) has not been assigned; therefore, 98 has not been added to the base number. Neither of the class numbers is below or above the limits of the class-number range.

When several classes printed on the same page require the use of the same Table of Geographical Divisions, one footnote serves all. The base numbers in the footnote are listed in the order that the class numbers appear on the page. Match the base numbers with the first numbers of each range. The three sets of class numbers in Example 3, shown without their subarrangements, are printed on the same page in the schedule.

EXAMPLE 3

Labor
Industrial hygiene. Welfare work.

HD7291-7390	Housing. By region or country. Table I[1]
HD7411-7510	Model plants and factories. By region or country. Table I[1]
HD7531-7630	Model communities. By region or country. Table I[1]

---

1. For Table I, see pp. 331-340, in H-HJ. Add country number in table to 7290, 7410, or 7530, as the case requires.

EXAMPLE 3, continued
_____

OBSERVE

1. The same geographical table applies to each of the three sets of range numbers.

2. One footnote suffices for the three class-number ranges.

3. The three base numbers correspond to the first numbers of the ranges and each base number is one less than its first range number.

_____

ALPHABETICAL ORDER OF GEOGRAPHICAL DIVISIONS

The signal for alphabetical order, A-Z, follows the geographical authorization caption. The letters indicate that the places are to be represented in call numbers by cutter numbers taken from their names. Alphabetization of locations in this way assembles in one place works pertinent to a subject in a particular area. The request for alphabetical order may be made at any level of geographical subdivision.

Customarily, single class numbers are allocated when geographical divisions are to be arranged alphabetically and the place names are omitted. The work of the classifier or shelflister is facilitated by three tables appended to the schedule: Table of Regions and Countries in One Alphabet, Table of States I, and Table of Cities in the United States. Arranged alphabetically by the names designated in their titles, these tables present preassigned cutter numbers for the places. The introductory paragraph to the Table of Regions and Countries states that the cutter numbers should not be regarded as fixed, since it may be necessary to adjust them to conform with particular shelflist situations. The statement is also applicable to the other two tables. To use any one of the three tables requires only the instruction A-Z after the geographical authorization. Alphabetical subarrangement is illustrated by Example 4.

EXAMPLE 4
_____

	Railways
	Railway administration
	Accidents
HE1779	General works
	By region or country
	United States
1780	General works
.5	By state, A-W
1781	By city, A-Z

59

EXAMPLE 4, continued
_____

1783	Other regions or countries, A-Z	
	Under each country:	
	.A1-5	Official reports
	.A6-Z	Nonofficial works

OBSERVE

1. The authorization caption, By region or country, introduces geographical subdivision.

2. United States has been developed in the schedule using single class numbers for each subdivision.

3. States and cities are to be assigned cutter numbers from their names.

4. The states and cities are not listed.

5. A single class number is provided for the territorial divisions Other regions or countries.

6. The other regions or countries are not listed.

7. A-Z calls for subarrangement by the cutter numbers of the other regions and countries.

_____

The cutter numbers for state, city, and country in the following Example 4 class numbers were taken from the appropriate tables.

HE1780.5	
.I8	Iowa
HE1781	
.S62	Sioux City, Iowa
HE1783	
.I4	India

For official reports on railway accidents in India, the assignment of dedicated cutter numbers is illustrated by the following call numbers selected from among thirty entries for India in the Library of Congress Shelflist:

HE1783	HE1783	HE1783	HE1783	HE1783	HE1783
.I4A475	.I4A478	.I4A479	.I4A4795	.I4A48	.I4A487
HE1783	HE1783	HE1783	HE1783	HE1783	HE1783
.I4A4993	.I4A4995	.I4A5	.I4A53	.I4A54	.I4A55

Cuttering geographical areas may present a problem if a place name has changed or if names are inverted. Guidelines for "current geographical conditions" and for inverted names have been set forth by Library of Congress in its Cataloging Service Bulletin.[5]

CLASSIFIED ORDER OF GEOGRAPHICAL DIVISIONS

Classified order occurs in two ways: locations to which the subject applies are enumerated in the schedule or a Table of Geographical Divisions is stated. Classified order is probably best seen in the Tables. The central column is composed of the territorial divisions of the world listed in a preferred order. That order is reflected to a large extent in enumerative displays. Sometimes both approaches serve the same subject.

Enumeration in the Schedule

When geographical subdivisions are enumerated under a subject in the schedule, the presentation sequence is: 1. the authorization caption, By region or country; 2. an internal table, if there is one; 3. the classified list of places; and 4. a class number or number range preceding each place. Exact classified order as in the Tables of Geographical Divisions is not necessarily strictly followed. The subject itself governs the order and extent of its geographical subdivisions.

The extent of enumeration may vary from continents only, with some exceptions, to a full array of appropriate areas. There may be more than one internal table, each applying to the places which follow. In partial listings, the remaining locations are assigned a Table of Geographical Divisions or alphabetical order. The most frequent separation is between the United States and other countries. Under Banking, By region or country, subdivisions for the United States are printed in the schedule between HG2401-2626. Other regions and countries are assigned the range span HG2701-3542.6, a Table of Geographical Divisions, and an internal table for their subdivisions.

It is possible in enumerative display to provide for geographical divisions that are not included in the Tables of Geographical Divisions. One place omitted from the Tables is Tuvalu, which shows at HJ98.7 (Public finance. Documents) in a classified list. Other Table omissions that have schedule notations are the Tropics and some associated countries.

Local development in enumerations is introduced by terms denoting local subdivision such as By state, By city, By province. Individual states and regions within the borders of the United States have been listed in the schedule a number of times. Those of other countries are rarely individualized in that way. Subdivision techniques for localities are described in Part 2, Geographical Divisions.

The class numbers HJ241-1620 (Local finance. History and conditions) illustrate some of the variations in enumerative display. Geographical divisions are listed in the schedule through Balkan States. Subdivisions for the United States, Canada, and Latin America are printed in the schedule beneath their names. Subdivisions for Central and South America are provided in separate internal tables. Subdivisions for European countries are printed for each country. The remaining places are assigned to a Table of Geographical Divisions and subdivisions are in an internal table. The way to apply classified schedule enumerations to internal tables is explained in Chapter 5, Internal Tables. The process is one of matching two sets of numbers.

Tables of Geographical Divisions

The second method of classified arrangement is achieved by the citation of one of the Tables of Geographical Divisions. The places are listed in the Table.

Ten tables, designated by Roman numerals, are distributed around a central list of world land areas arranged in a preferred or classified order in four levels. Continents and other major geographical areas form the first level. The order of these is America, North America, Latin America, Europe, Asia, Africa, Atlantic Ocean Islands, Indian Ocean Islands, Australia, New Zealand, Pacific Ocean Islands, Arctic regions, and Antarctic regions. Latin America as a geographical unit is somewhat different from other first-level land forms. Europe, Indian Ocean Islands, etc., are recognizable in their names as specific types of geographical divisions. Latin America draws upon languages for its identity and unites in its name diverse land areas as this definition states:

> ...the Spanish-speaking, Portuguese-speaking, and French-speaking countries (except Canada) of North America, South America, Central America, and the West Indies. The term is also used to include Puerto Rico, the French West Indies, and other islands of the West Indies where a romance language is spoken. Occasionally the term is used to include British Honduras, Guyana, French Guiana, and Surinam. [6]

Regions larger than a country, countries, associated countries, and islands appropriate to each first-level division make up the other three levels of the Tables. For the most part, countries are arranged alphabetically under continents and regions. The names of local areas—cities, counties, etc.—are not included. The United States is unique in that regions within its borders are named in the Tables and states and cities are provided for alphabetically.

In each Table, a certain span of numbers from one to twenty is assigned to each location. Table II, for example, provides one and two numbers for each place. The absence of numbers for the United States, with one exception, in Tables VI-X indicates that those Tables do not apply to the United States. Each table also has a different set of total numbers which can be ascertained by examining the last number of the Table; but that is misleading. The totals are greater because many numbers have been expanded decimally in order to accommodate all places.

The Tables supply the former names of places, the current name preceding the former. Examples with Table I numbers are 17.5, Belize, formerly British Honduras; 69.8, Sri Lanka, formerly Ceylon; and 85.5, Zaire, formerly Democratic Republic of the Congo.

Some places in the Tables have been relocated. Where relocations have occurred, a see reference is given to the correct number in Table I. Hawaii, for example, once considered a Pacific Ocean Island and now a constituent of the United States, has the reference See 13, placing it with States, A-W. Presently, other relocations are Greenland, Burma, and Iceland.

Since publication of the fourth edition of Class H, several additions and changes have been made to the Tables. Gilbert Islands has been added to the central location column. Cambodia has been changed to Kampuchea and the French Territory of the Afars and Issas to the Republic of Djibouti. Luxemburg is to be spelled Luxembourg.

There is a single range of class numbers when a Table is quoted for geographical subdivision. The range precedes the authorization phrases By region or country or Other regions or countries. All the places in the Table to be included must be encompassed within that range. Geographical areas applicable to the subject which are not named in the Table are given class numbers in the schedule. Among omissions are the associated countries listed in Chapter 9, Countries. Local units are provided for by type in an accompanying internal table or by schedule class numbers.

The footnote indicated after Table numbers introduces the base number. The base number is required in building a class number.

When a Table is assigned, there may be, and often is, an accompanying internal table. Also, the term "modified" may be specified after the Table number, indicating that there are changes in the numbering system. The following subsections consider the construction of class numbers: 1. when an internal table is not involved, 2. when there is an internal table, and 3. when a Table is modified.

Without Internal Tables. Example 5 is typical of provisions when an internal table does not accompany the citation of a Table of Geographical Divisions. Table I, in which one number is assigned to each location, is the Table most frequently cited.

EXAMPLE 5

```
                Railways
                  Railway administration
                    Rates.  Tariff
                      Cf.  HE2301+, Freight
HE1831                General works
   1836               General special
   1841-1940          By region or country.  Table I[1]
```

1. For Table, See pp. 331-340, H-HJ. Add country number in table to 1840, 2000, or 2120, as the case requires.

OBSERVE

1. Table I is cited.
2. An internal table is not provided.

PROCEDURE

In the absence of an internal table, constructing a class number follows the two main steps described for base numbers. The steps can be restated as an equation. Below the equation, the numbers for Canada are displayed.

	country number from the Table	+	base number	=	class number
Canada	14	+	1840	=	1854

The class number for Canada in Example 5, then, is HE1854. As an internal table is lacking, nothing further but a cutter number is required. Note that the class number falls within the assignable number range preceding By region or country.

With Internal Tables. Internal tables are regularly displayed in the schedule after the geographical caption and Table number; however, a table printed for one subject may also serve another subject. In that case, a Subarranged like note refers to the model internal table. Internal tables provide the subdivision structure for subjects and are so organized that their sequential numbers equal the range numbers in the stated Tables.

PROCEDURE

To form a class number, the two sets of numbers must be matched. Use these steps:
1. Determine the form, topic, or other aspect treated in the work.
2. Locate the country in the central column of the Tables.
3. Find the number(s) opposite the country in the Table cited.
4. Determine the range of numbers assigned to the country in the Table.
5. Find the column in the internal table which matches the range of country numbers.
6. Select the sequential number in parentheses in the column opposite the form, topic, or other subdivision determined in no. 1.
7. Determine the number in the range of numbers assigned to the country which

EXAMPLE 5, continued
_____

corresponds to the sequential number selected in no. 6.

8. Add the number from no. 7 to the base number given in the footnote.

The resulting class number should fall within the span of numbers assigned to the subject in the schedule. The steps are illustrated in Example 6.

EXAMPLE 6
_____

Economic history and conditions
   Land use
      By region or country
HD311-1130.5   Other regions or countries. Table VII, modified[1]
          Under each country:

10 nos.	5 nos.	1 no.	
(1).A1A-Z	(1)	.A1A-Z	Periodicals. Serials
(1.5)	(1.5)	.A5A-Z	Societies
	(3)	.A6-Z6	History
			Including policy
(3)			General works
(4)			Early
(5)			19th and 20th centuries
(6)	(3.2)	.Z63A-Z	1945-
(8)		.Z7A-Z	Special. Miscellaneous
			Local
			Including real estate
(9)	(4)	.Z8A-Z	By region or state, A-Z
(10)	(5)	.Z9A-Z	By city, etc., A-Z

              Note: Great Britain
              594.6   Enclosures
                .8   18th century
              644.8   France. 18th century

_____
1. For Table VII, see pp. 331-340 in H-HJ. Add country number in table to 300.

OBSERVE
_____

1. The class number range precedes the geographical instruction.

2. A Table is cited and it is to be modified. (The Table does not apply to the United States).

3. An internal table is provided.

4. The range columns of the internal table match the range spans assigned to countries in Table VII.

5. Local areas have been provided for in the internal table.

Combining a Table of Geographical Divisions with an internal table to form a class number is demonstrated using Example 6. The subject is land use; the country is Great Britain.

Step 1

The particular aspect is history of land use during the 17th century.

Step 2

Great Britain is under Europe in the Tables of Geographical Divisions.

Step 3

Table VII allocates 291-300 to Great Britain.

Step 4

291-300 is a range of ten numbers.

Step 5

The column headed 10 nos. in the internal table matches the number range of Great Britain.

Step 6

Under the subdivision History, the 17th century is covered by Early at sequential number (4) in the 10 nos. column.

Step 7

The fourth number in Great Britain's range is 294.

Step 8

The base number in the footnote is 300; 294 plus 300 equals 594, making HD594 the class number for 17th century history of land use in Great Britain.

Modification Annotation. The word "modified" appearing after a Table citation "indicates that following the 'Under Each' statement are special provisions to be used in the particular spread of numbers."[7] Within country ranges, Table numbers are adjusted by decimal extensions and given special meanings to fit the needs of individual countries. The modifications may be introduced by the word Note and given in tabular form after the internal table as in Example 6, or they may be in paragraphs as for HF1451-1647 (Commercial policy). The general modification pattern consists of 1. the names of the geographical areas, 2. the modified class numbers, and 3. the special topics of the class numbers. The note in Example 6 exemplifies the characteristics of modifications.

If the work described in the steps for Example 6 had been about 18th century land use history of Great Britain, the class number 594.8 from the modification note would have been the proper one. By means of the decimal extension, 18th century history is retained in early history but is set apart as a special aspect of the historical period. The modifications for Great Britain have been inserted in the following complete range of its class numbers. Note that the two numbers fit into the range without further alterations. Note also that they cannot be represented by sequential numbering in the 10 nos. column of the internal table because of their special relationship to a single country.

10 nos.	Great Britain's Numbers	
(1)	HD591	Periodicals. Serials
(1.5)	591.5	Societies
		History
(3)	593	General works
(4)	594	Early
Modifications	} 594.6	Enclosures
inserted	} 594.8	18th century
(5)	595	19th and 20th centuries
(6)	596	1945-
(8)	598	Special. Miscellaneous
		Local
(9)	599	By region or state, A-Z
(10)	600	By city, etc., A-Z

The phrases Unless otherwise provided for and Except for the United States may be a part of the Under each instructions. Those phrases also indicate modification. Such a modification shows for the United States at HE9801-9900 (Air transportation) where the modification is in a note.

Two variations on standard modification form should be noted. The first variant presents the special provisions as class numbers in the schedule rather than in a note. Table I, modified, is assigned to Foreign commerce, With other regions, at HF3065-3150. In place of the range numbers in Table I for regions, states and cities of the United States, class numbers between HF3151-3163 (Local commerce) have been given to those geographical areas. The regions listed include only those bordering on principal waterways. The second variation occurs at HD2981-3110.9 (Industrial cooperation). The modification is made to the internal table for HD3441-3750.7 (Cooperative distribution) which HD2981+ is to be subarranged like. The modification revises the sequential indications for Local.

ALPHABETICAL-CLASSIFIED COMBINATIONS

When classified and alphabetical order are combined: 1. the places listed are usually continents and other large areas; 2. the places are given in classified order; 3. each area is assigned one class number (the United States is often exempted from that restriction), and 4. regions and countries are to be subarranged by their cutter numbers under the parent geographical area. The excerpt in Example 6 displays alphabetical and classified order united under a subject.

EXAMPLE 7

Public finance
  Claims
    By region or country
      Under each country (using successive Cutter numbers):
        .x   Periodicals. Societies. Serials
        .x2 General works. Principles
        .x3 Administration
        .x4 Special claims
      For claims which are of primary interest in connection with
        a special subject, see the subject
      For foreign claims, e.g. claims by citizens or government
        of one country against government or citizens of another
        country, see JX238+; JX351+
      United States

HJ	8931	Periodicals. Societies. Serials
	8932	Lists
	8933	General works
	8934	Administration
	8936	Special claims, A-Z
	8941	By region or state, A-Z
	8943	Confederate States
	8945	Canada
	8949	Latin America. By region or country, A-Z
		Including West Indies
	8951	Europe. By region or country, A-Z
	8953	Asia. By region or country, A-Z
	8957	Australia
	8959	New Zealand
	8963	Pacific Islands, A-Z

OBSERVE

1. The geographical divisions are listed in classified order.

2. The United States has several topical class numbers.

3. One class number identifies each of the other geographical divisions.

4. A-Z authorizes alphabetization of regions and countries under the geographical divisions with one class number.

The ten Tables of Geographical Divisions have been cited over 100 times in the H schedule. The largest number of the Tables is assigned to Other regions or countries.

NOTES

1. Nicholas Hedlesky, "Special Problems in Social and Political Sciences (Classes H and J)," in The Use of the Library of Congress Classification; Proceedings of the Institute on the Use of the Library of Congress Classification, ed. by Richard H. Schimmelpfeng and C. Donald Cook (Chicago: American Library Association, 1968), p. 37.

2. Lois M. Chan, Immroth's Guide to the Library of Congress Classification, 3rd ed. (Littleton, Colo.: Libraries Unlimited, 1980), p. 182.

3. Leo E. LaMontagne, American Library Classification with Special Reference to the Library of Congress Classification (Hamden, Conn.: Shoe String Press, 1961), p. 284.

4. Cataloging Service Bulletin 21:78 (Summer 1983).

5. Cataloging Service Bulletin 21:79 (Summer 1983).

6. International Geographic Encyclopedia and Atlas (Boston: Houghton Mifflin, 1979), p. 406.

7. Hedlesky, p. 45.

part two
geographical divisions

chapter 8
regions

The general formula for regional subdivision is the phrase By region or country—the authorizing phrase for all geographical subdivision. Regions can mean those larger than a country, those of an individual country, or those of an individual state. This chapter reviews the major means of subdivision for regions larger than a country, regions of the United States, and regions of other countries, as well as the Arctic and Antarctic regions, the Tropics, and special regions.

REGIONS LARGER THAN A COUNTRY

By region or country followed by A-Z without a listing of the geographical areas means that cutter numbers are to be derived from the names of regions larger than a country or the names of individual countries. That holds true even if subject headings have local units as subdivisions. Cuttering for localities within a country requires further subarrangement.[1]

The Table of Regions and Countries in One Alphabet supplies some regional names with suggested cutter numbers. The Table would be used with Examples 1 and 2.

EXAMPLE 1

	Social pathology. Social and public welfare.
	Criminology
	Medical charities
	Social services to the sick
HV 687.A2	Periodicals. Societies. Serials
.A3-Z	General works
.5	By region or country, A-Z

73

EXAMPLE I, continued
_____

OBSERVE

1. A decimally extended class number has been assigned to regions and countries.

2. The regions are not named.

3. The first cutter number is to be assigned from the names of the regions or countries.

_____

_____

EXAMPLE 2
_____

                Labor exchanges. Employment agencies. State employment
                            bureaus, etc.

HD 5860   Periodicals. Societies. Serials
    5861   General works
    5870   By industry or trade, A-Z[2]

                Under each:

                    .x   General works
                    .x2   By region or country, A-Z

_____

1. For a list of industries and trades, <u>see</u> pp. 88-96 in H-HJ. Use insofar as applicable.

OBSERVE

1. In the successive cutter-number pattern, regional cutter numbers are secondary to those for industries and trades.

2. Regions and countries are to be arranged in alphabetical order.

_____

      For classified order, regions are enumerated in the schedule among other geographical divisions in the established order or a Table of Geographical Divisions is designated. In the Tables, regions are defined by the countries listed beneath them. In classified enumerations, regions are sometimes defined as they are for Scandinavia and Middle East at HC341-380 and HC415.15-415.4 (Economic history and conditions). An entirely different approach to regions larger than a country in a classified sequence is shown in Example 3.

EXAMPLE 3

Utilization and culture of special classes of lands
Water resources development. Water supply
By region or country
Other American regions or countries

HD 1696   By country, A-Z

Under each:
.x   General works
.x2   International questions. By date
.x3   By state, A-Z
.x4   Other local, A-Z

.5   Regions (not limited to one country), A-Z
                 e.g. .R5 Rio de la Plata region

Europe
1697.A5   General works
.A6-Z   By country, A-Z
                 Subarranged like HD1696

.5   Regions (not limited to one country), A-Z
                 e.g. .T3 Tagus Valley

OBSERVE

1. Regions and countries are separated.

2. Regions have been assigned to a single class number.

3. Regions are defined as larger than an individual country.

4. At each class number for regions, an e.g. note gives the name and cutter number of a region as an example. Otherwise, no regions are listed.

Two other examples of the regions not limited to one country were found in the Library of Congress Shelflist for HD1697.5: Socca Valley and Rhine River Watershed.

        Between HC240-246 (Economic history and conditions), individual class numbers have been assigned to two types of regions larger than a country. The names of the regions in the first type — Northern Europe, Central Europe, etc. — establish their position on the continent. The names of regions in the second type — European Economic Community, European Free Trade Association — represent individual countries united by mutual concerns. As regional groups, the second type qualifies for this chapter and section. As countries, the second type also qualifies for Chapter 9, Countries, where they have been included among others of a similar kind under the heading Associated Countries.

REGIONS OF THE UNITED STATES

As is often the case, the United States is separated from other countries and its subdivisions are given directly under its name. Regions of the United States have been singled out as one of the subdivisions. Provisions are made for regions covering more than one state and for regions within individual states.

Regions Larger than a State

Three general methods are employed to indicate subarrangements for regions larger than a state. Regions are: 1. enumerated in the schedule, 2. grouped with other local units, and 3. named in the Tables of Geographical Divisions. In addition to these three general methods, there is a fourth method that is used occasionally. A parenthetical phrase limiting regions to those covering more than one state is placed after the caption. Two entries where that occurs are HA218 (Statistical data) and at the span HJ276-279 (Public finance. History and conditions). No regions are listed at HA 218. Not only are regions named at the span of class numbers, but they are given dedicated cutter numbers for their subdivisions.

Regions Enumerated in the Schedule   In the first method of handling regions of the United States, individual regions are listed in the schedule. There are several different regional groups. Examples 4, 5, and 6 show three of the groups. Note the wide variation in the names and number of the regions in each example. Note also that in Example 5, regions are called interstate while another form of regional division, metropolitan areas, is introduced.

EXAMPLE 4

	Automotive transportation
	By region or country
	United States
	By region
HE 5624	New England
5625	Middle Atlantic States
5626	South
5627	North Central
5628	Mississippi Valley
5629	West
5630	Southwest, New
5631	Pacific Coast states
5632	Other, A-Z
5633	By state, A-W
5634	By city, A-Z
5635-5720	←Other regions or countries. Table I[1]

---

1. For Table I, see pp. 331-340 in H-HJ. Add country number in Table to 5620 or 5270, as the case requires.

EXAMPLE 4, continued

OBSERVE

1. The geographical development of the United States is separated from that of other countries.

2. There are eight named regions, each with an individual class number.

3. If there are additional regions, they are to be classed in the ninth number arranged by their cutter numbers.

CHAPTER 5

Communities. Classes. Races
Urban groups. The city. Urban sociology
Regional planning
By region or country
United States

HT 392	General works
.5	By interstate region, A-Z
	For interstate metropolitan areas, see HT394
.A7	Appalachian region
.A8	Atlantic States
.C42	Lake Champlain region
.C45	Chesapeake Bay region
.G7	Great Lakes Region
.G74	Great Plains
.M54	Minnesota-Wisconsin
.M6	Mo-Kan
.N4	New England
.P3	Pacific Northwest
.P4	Penjerdel
.P6	Potomac Valley
.S65	Southern States
.T3	Lake Tahoe region
.T46	Tennessee Valley
.T7	Tri-State region (New York, New Jersey, Connecticut)
393	By state, A-W
	Under each:
.x	General
.x2	Local, A-Z
394	By metropolitan area, A-Z
395	Other regions or countries, A-Z
	Under each country:
.x	General works
.x2	By region, province, state, etc., A-Z
.x3	By metropolitan area, A-Z

EXAMPLE 5, continued
_____

OBSERVE

1. A single class number is assigned to regions.

2. Fourteen regions are listed alphabetically, each with topical cutter numbers.

3. States in the Tri-State region are named.

_____

Two interstate regions have been added to HT392.5: Delaware Valley, .D4 and New York Bight Region, .N45. The Library of Congress Shelflist shows the following metropolitan areas on catalog entries for HT394: Baltimore metropolitan area, Boston metropolitan area, New York metropolitan area, Philadelphia metropolitan area, St. Louis metropolitan area, San Francisco metropolitan area, Savannah metropolitan area, Twin Cities metropolitan area, Washington metropolitan area.

EXAMPLE 6
_____

Local finance
  By region or country
    United States
     Regions
      Under each:

	(0) or (5)		General (including works on the budget and expenditure)
			History. By period
	(1)	(6).A3A-Z	Through 1860
		.A5-Z	1861-
	(2)	(7)	Taxation
	(3)	(8)	Credit. Debt. Loans
	(4)	(9)	Administration
HJ 9170-9174	New England and Atlantic States		
9175-9179	Southern States		
9180-9184	Middle Western States		
9185-9189	Pacific States		

OBSERVE

1. The word Regions introduces regional subdivision.

2. Five regions are named.

3. A five-number double-column internal table provides sequential numbers to match the five class numbers assigned to each region.

_____

Regions Grouped With Other Local Units. In the second method of handling regions of the United States, regions as subdivisions are paired in the caption with states in one class number or are combined with other local units. This method is similar to the first method in that a list of regions is provided, but the list appears in the Table of Regions in the United States appended to the schedule. Ironically, the geographical direction requests alphabetical order while the Table presents the regions in logical order. Twenty regions are established in the Table with the assigned range of dedicated cutter numbers .A1-195. Three regions have been added to the Table. They are:

North Central States. Middle West	.A14
Ohio Valley	.A16
Sunbelt States	.A163

The dedicated cutter numbers in the Table of Regions precede the first state cutter number, .A2, Alabama, in Table of States I, thereby avoiding a conflict in the pairing of regions and states in the same class number. According to the introductory statement at the head of the Table of Regions in Volume H-HJ, two standard patterns call for assignment of the dedicated cutter numbers in the Table. One pattern is set forth in Example 7, the other in Example 8. The excerpt in Example 8 is a standard pattern for subarrangement of localities.

EXAMPLE 7

```
                    Crimes and offenses
                      Political crimes
                        Offenses against the government
                          National
                            By region or country
                              United States
HV  6285                       General works
    6288                       By region or state, A-Z
    6289                       By city, A-Z
    6295                     ←Other regions or countries, A-Z
                               Under each country:

                                 .x    General works
                                 .x2   Local, A-Z
```

OBSERVE

1. Subdivisions for the United States have been assigned class numbers in the schedule.
2. Regions and states have been given one class number.
3. The pattern of By region or state, A-Z, following General works indicates that regions of the United States are to be assigned the dedicated cutter numbers from the Table of Regions in the United States.

EXAMPLE 8

> The family. Marriage. Home
> Free love
> Particular communities
> HQ 967   By region or country, A-Z
>
> Under each country:
> .x   General works
> .x2   Local, A-Z

OBSERVE

1. Local, A-Z, at .x2 means that a second cutter number is to represent the local areas of each country, including regions.

2. For the United States, General works followed by Local, A-Z, in the successive cutter number subarrangement means that the dedicated cutter numbers from the Table of Regions in the United States are to be assigned under .x2.

Regions in the Tables of Geographical Divisions. In the third method of handling regions of the United States, a Table of Geographical Divisions is assigned to the caption. Only Tables I-V can be applied to the United States because the other five tables lack range numbers for the United States. There is a span of numbers for Pacific States in Table X but it has not been assigned under the United States. Inclusion in Tables I-V is limited as, most frequently, they are used to furnish the names of other regions and countries. Even if the Table is not for other geographical divisions only, the United States can be excluded from the Table by a note, an exception phrase, or printed subdivisions.

Conveying regional subdivision by Tables I-IV is the same as the first method. There is a list of regions. The distinction is in the placement of the regions in the Tables where range numbers have been assigned to yet a different set of regions. The United States is to be included in By region or country, A-Z, at HE2001-2100 (Railway administration. Traffic. Rates). Neither a phrase, a note, nor subdivisions indicate exemption from the Table's provisions.

In Table V, there are no range numbers opposite names of the regions. Instead, United States has been given a four-number span. The citation of Table V requires an Under each subarrangement that includes regions in some way. Illustrative are HV4761-4890.7 (Protection of animals), with the subdivision By region or state in the internal table, and HS201-330.7 (Secret societies), with Local as a subdivision.

In-State Regions

For regions within state lines, the geographical authorization By region or state, A-Z, must have an Under each state subarrangement providing for localities. The subarrangement usually presents successive cutter numbers. One example is HD8011 (State labor. Administrative (and industrial)) where .x2 is captioned By country, region, etc.

Regions within the borders of individual states are also provided for in the Tables of Geographical Divisions. Following the enumeration of regions larger than a state in the central column of the Tables, there is a line for States, A-W. Beneath States, A-W, a note indicates that regions are to be included. As with regions larger than a state, only Tables I-V apply to in-state regions.

REGIONS OF OTHER COUNTRIES

Provisions for regions within a country conform to general patterns of subdivision. The excerpts in Examples 9, 10, and 11 are from classified enumerations. Example 9, in which a partial list of continents continues those in Example 3, displays an Under each country statement with a subdivision for Local and a Subarranged like note. Subdivisions are developed under individual countries in Examples 10 and 11; in Example 11 the exceptional occurs.

EXAMPLE 9

Utilization and culture of special classes of lands
Water resources development.   Water supply
By region or country
Asia

HD 1698.A1A-Z	General works
.A2-Z	By region or country

Under each country:

.x	General works
.x2	Local, A-Z

1699	Africa

Subarranged like HD1698

OBSERVE

1. Continents are arranged in classified order.
2. Countries must be within the continents named.
3. Local, A-Z, in the subarrangement provides for the regions of each country.
4. Subdivisions of Africa follow the pattern under Asia.

EXAMPLE 10

```
                        Public finance
                          Revenue.  Taxation
                            By region or country
                              Europe
                                Italy
HJ  2741                          General works
                                  History.   By period
     2742                           Medieval
     2744                           17th and 18th centuries.
     2746                           Early 19th century, through 1861
                                    Modern
     2762                             General works
     2763                             1861-1900
     2765                             1901-
     2767                             Special
     2773                        Regions, provinces, A-Z
```

OBSERVE

The geographical subdivision for the country pairs regions with provinces in one class number.

EXAMPLE 11

```
                        Commerce
                          History
                            By period
                              Middle Ages (476-1400/1492)
                                By region or country
                                  Germany
HF  441                             General works
     442                            General special
                                      e.g.  The mercantile houses:  Fugger, Welser
                                    By place
     444                              South Germany.  Danube River region
     450                              Rhine River region
     453                              Other local, A-Z
```

OBSERVE

Some regions of one country are named in the schedule.

The frequency with which subdivisions of the United States have been assigned class numbers in the schedule leaves the remaining countries to be handled by subarrangements under the caption Other regions or countries. The countries in Table I for HV7315-7400 (Penology) are to be subdivided By region or state, A-Z, in a dedicated cutter-number series. Example 5 in this chapter displays successive cutter numbers at HT395 for Other regions or countries. By region, province, state, etc., A-Z, is assigned to .x2. The list which follows presents some of the regions found on catalog entries in the Library of Congress Shelflist for HT395.x2.

Countries	Regions
Australia	Flinders range region
Austria	Austria, Lower; Austria, Upper
Belgium	Flanders, East; Flanders, West; Louvain region
Brazil	Crato region
Canada	Winnipeg region
Denmark	Frederik sound region
France	Lyons region; Loire Valley; Grenoble region; Rhone Valley
Ireland	Banbridge region
Italy	Valle d'Aosta (region)
Japan	Lake Bewa region
Norway	Oslo region
Venezuela	Aroa Valley
Yugoslavia	Adriatic Sea region

ARCTIC AND ANTARCTIC REGIONS

As main land areas, the Arctic and Antarctic regions, the last two geographical divisions in the Tables of Geographical Divisions, are on a level with continents and are included whereever a Table is quoted. In the body of the schedule, the two regions may be given individual class numbers as at HA4020 and HA4020.5 (Statistical data).

THE TROPICS

Recognition as a geographical unit has not been granted to the Tropics in the Tables of Geographical Divisions. The Tropics have been named in the schedule in at least one place. In the enumerative display for Economic history and conditions, HC695 is captioned Tropics.

SPECIAL REGIONS

Regions considered in the category of Special regions have one main distinction. They relate principally to water areas. Only two or three subjects have Special regions, of which Example 12 is one.

EXAMPLE 12

	Telecommunication industry. Telegraph
	Submarine telegraph. Ocean cables
HE 7713	By region or country, A-Z
	Special regions
7725	Atlantic cables
7731	Pacific cables
7741	Other, A-Z

OBSERVE

1.   The regions are labelled special.

2.   Two regions are named.

Another Special region is the North Atlantic region. It has been assigned the class number HF4045 at the end of an internal table for Commerce, Other regions or countries. The region has not been named anywhere else and because it is not in the Tables of Geographical Divisions it must follow the internal table along with Communist countries.

NOTE

1.   Cataloging Service Bulletin 21:79 (Summer 1983).

chapter 9
countries

Authorization for subdivision by country is coupled with regions. The overall direction, By region or country, includes the countries of the world to which the subject applies. A secondary direction, Other regions or countries, excludes those countries treated in the schedule immediately following the general authorization. The obsolete phrase, By country, has not been deleted entirely from the H schedule. Interpret the phrase to mean By region or country unless instructions state otherwise or there is good reason not to. By country is required at HD1696 and HD1697.A6–Z (Water resources development. Water supply) because regions and countries are assigned to separate class numbers.

Some common features of subdivision by country are: 1. the order is either alphabetical, classified, or a combination of the two; 2. in classified listings, countries are usually subsumed under continents and may also be under regions or associated countries; 3. the United States is frequently set apart from other countries and given more extensive treatment; 4. othe countries may all be listed in the schedule, partially listed, or omitted entirely; and 5. provisions for sub-divisions include dedicated cutter numbers, successive cutter numbers, Subarranged like, and internal tables. Under the headings Alphabetical Order and Classified Order, a sampling of patterns of subdivision by country is presented. Countries grouped together for various reasons or that have joined together to achieve common purposes are listed in a third section captioned Associated Countries.

ALPHABETICAL ORDER OF COUNTRIES

Alphabetical order is obtained by cutter numbers built on the initial letters of country names attached to the class number as a first cutter number. Collocation by country under a subject is thus achieved. It is characteristic of alphabetical order for the class number to be a single one and to omit the names of the countries. An alphabetical list of countries has been supplied with preassigned cutter numbers in an appended table, the Table of Regions and Countries in One

Alphabet. Russia has been changed to Soviet Union, .S64, in the Table. The Table of Regions and Countries is not cited with the caption but is to be used whenever the direction states By region or country, A-Z, or Other regions or countries, A-Z. Use the Table to assign the country cutter numbers in Examples 1, 2, and 3.

EXAMPLE 1

Children.   Child development
Child life (Descriptive).   Activities of childhood
HQ 792   Social conditions of children.   By region or country, A-Z

OBSERVE

1.   No countries are excluded by the geographical instruction.
2.   The countries are not named.
3.   The first cutter number is to be for the name of the country.
4.   No further subdivision of the countries has been provided.

EXAMPLE 2

Crimes and offenses
Crimes against persons
Suicide
HV 6548   By region or country, A-Z
Under each country:

.x   General works
.x2   Local, A-Z

OBSERVE

1.   HV6548 is to be assigned to a work on any country.
2.   Names of countries are omitted.
3.   Countries are to be cuttered by their names as indicated by A-Z after the direction to subdivide geographically.
4.   The Under each country subarrangement is a general pattern.

86

EXAMPLE 3

```
                        Protection, assistance and relief
                          Special classes
                            Immigrants
                              By region or country
                                United States
        HV 4010                     General works
           4011                     By region or state, A-Z
           4012                     By city, A-Z
           4013                   Other regions and countries, A-Z
```

OBSERVE

1. Subdivisions of the United States have been allotted individual class numbers.
2. Countries other than the United States are to be designated in call numbers by cutter numbers representing their names.
3. Further subdivision of other countries is lacking.

CLASSIFIED ORDER OF COUNTRIES

Individual countries are printed in the schedule, each accompanied by a specific range of numbers, or are found in the Tables of Geographical Divisions. Countries are often referred to by the extent of the number range assigned to them in the schedule or in the Tables: one-number countries, two-number countries, etc. As in the Tables of Geographical Divisions, enumerated countries are subordinated to continents and regions, with some exceptions. The order of the countries, however, does not always reflect precisely that of the Tables.

Examples 4 and 5 employ the Tables of Geographical Divisions. Example 6 presents a full list of applicable countries printed in the schedule in classified order. In Example 7, first-level geographical divisions have not been supplied for some countries. Example 8 displays alphabetical order combined with classified order and an internal table containing a cutter-number range-column.

EXAMPLE 4

```
                     Labor
                       Classes of labor
                         Woman labor
        HD 6091-6220.7       By region or country.   Table V$^2$
```

Under each country:

4 nos.	1 no.	
(1) .A1-5		Periodicals. Societies. Serials
(2) .A6-Z		Statistics
(3) .A7-Z5		General works
(4) .Z6A-Z		Local, A-Z
	6223	Underdeveloped areas.

2. For Table V, <u>see</u> pp. 331-340 in H-HJ. Add country number in table to 6090.

OBSERVE

1. Countries are not listed but none are excluded.

2. The Table citation accompanying the geographical direction indicates the Table of Geographical Divisions to be used and where the names of the countries will be found.

3. Provisions for form, topical, or other subdivisions of the subject are provided by an internal table.

4. The base number is one less than the first number of the class-number range.

EXAMPLE 5

		Transportation and communications
		Express service - Continued
HE	5886	Public policy (General)
	5889	Rates
		By region or country
		United States
	5893	Periodicals. Societies
	5895	Directories
	5896	General works
	5898	Public policy
	5900	Administration. Operation. The express business
		For comparative express and parcel post rates, <u>see</u> HE6473
	5902	Finance. Accounting
	5903	Individual companies, A-Z
		Under each:

	.x1-49	Periodicals. Serials
	.x5A-Z	General works

	5904	By state, A-Z
	.5	By city, A-Z

EXAMPLE 5, continued

5905-5990	Other regions or countries. Table I[1]
	Under each country:

       .AI-39   Periodicals. Societies. Serials
       .A4   General works
       .A5-Z7   Individual companies, A-Z

1. For Table I, see pp. 331-340 in H-HJ. Add country number in table to 5890.

OBSERVE

1. The separation of the United States and the allocation of schedule class numbers to its subdivisions is characteristic.

2. For those countries other than the United States a range of numbers has been assigned.

3. Table I of the Tables of Geographical Divisions supplies the names of the other countries.

4. For other countries, subarrangement is in the form of dedicated cutter numbers.

5. The base number is more than one less than the first range number.

EXAMPLE 6

Public finance
  Documents. By country
    United States
      Serial reports, and special documents
HJ 11   By state, A-W
          For District of Columbia appropriations, etc.,
            see HJ9013.W2; HJ9215+
          Under each (local terminology may vary):
            .x   Report of the treasurer or finance
                 department
            .x2   Report of the auditor; or comptroller
            .x4   Budget
            .x5   Report of the revenue/tax commissioner
            .x6   Report of the assessors
            .x7   Report of the state board of equalization
            .x8   Report of the commissioner of excise
            .x9   Report of the commissioner of the sinking
                 fund
            .x95 Special documents. By date
    Other countries
      Under each:
        .AI-199 General reports of the department of
               finance or treasurer
        .A2-299 Budget
        .A3-399 Receipts and expenditures

EXAMPLE 6, continued
_____

		.A4-499	Public debt

.A4-499	Public debt
.A5-599	Administrative reports
	Including bureaus, special officers, etc.
.A7-799	Other. Miscellaneous
	e.g. Colonies
.A8-Z	Local (States, provinces, etc.)
	Cf. HJ9000+, Municipal finance

		Canada
12		To 1867
		Dominion of Canada
13.A1-6		General
.A8-Z		Provinces
		Latin America
15		Mexico
		Central America
16		General
.5		Belize
17		Costa Rica
18		Guatemala
19		Honduras
20		Nicaragua
21		Panama
22		Salvador
		West Indies
.5		Bahamas
23		Cuba
24		Puerto Rico
25		Haiti
26		Dominican Repubic. Santo Domingo
27		British West Indies
.3		Jamaica
28.3		Leeward Islands
.5		Windward Islands
.7		Trinidad and Tobago
29		Virgin Islands of the United States
.3		Netherlands Antilles. Dutch West Indies
		French West Indies
.5		Guadeloupe
.7		Martinique
		South America
30		Argentina
31		Bolivia
32		Brazil
33		Chile
34		Colombia
35		Ecuador
		Guianas
.3		Guyana. British Guiana
.5		Surinam. Dutch Guiana
.7		French Guiana
36		Paraguay
37		Peru
38		Uruguay
39		Venezuela

	Europe
	Great Britain
40	General
41	England and Wales
42.2	Northern Ireland
43	Scotland
.5	Ireland. Irish Republic
44	Austria
.5	Czechoslovakia
46	Hungary
47	France
48	Germany
	Including West Germany
49.5	East Germany
50	Greece
51	Italy
52.5	San Marino
.7	Malta
	Benelux countries. Low countries
53	Belgium
54	Netherlands
.5	Luxemburg, Luxembourg
55	Soviet Union
.3	Finland
.7	Poland
	Scandinavia
56	Denmark
57	Iceland
.5	Greenland
58	Norway
59	Sweden
60	Spain
.5	Gibraltar
61	Portugal
62	Switzerland
	Balkan States
63.3	Albania
.5	Bulgaria
.7	Yugoslavia
.9	Romania
	Asia
	Asia
	Middle East. Near East
64	Turkey
.2	Cyprus
.25	Syria
.3	Lebanon
.35	Israel. Palestine
.4	Jordan
.45	Saudi Arabia
.5	Yemen (Yemen Arab Republic)
.55	Yemen (People's Democratic Republic).
	Southern Yemen. Aden (Colony and Protectorate)
.6	United Arab Emirates. Trucial States
.65	Kuwait

.7	Iraq
.75	Iran
	South Asia
.8	Burma
.85	Sri Lanka
.9	Nepal
65	India
67.5	Pakistan
.8	Bangladesh
	Southeast Asia. Indochina
70.2	Cambodia
.3	Laos
.4	Vietnam
.6	Thailand
.7	Malaysia. Malaya
.8	Singapore
.9	Brunei
71.5	Indonesia
73	Philippines
	East Asia. Far East
77	Japan
.5	Korea
	Including South Korea
.55	North Korea
.6	China
.65	Macao
.7	Taiwan. Formosa
.75	Hongkong
	Africa
	North Africa
80.2	Morocco
.3	Algeria
.4	Tunisia
.5	Egypt. United Arab Republic
.6	Sudan
	Northeast Africa
.7	Ethiopia
.8	Somalia
	Including British and Italian Somaliland
81.2	French Territory of the Afars and Issas
	Southeast Africa
.3	Kenya
.4	Uganda
.5	Rwanda
.6	Burundi
.7	Tanzania. Tanganyika
.8	Mozambique
82.2	Madagascar
	Southern Africa
.3	South Africa
.4	Rhodesia
	Including Southern Rhodesia
.5	Zambia. Northern Rhodesia
.6	Lesotho. Basutoland
.7	Swaziland
.8	Botswana. Bechuanaland

EXAMPLE 6, continued
_____

83.2	Malawi. Nyasaland
.3	Namibia. Southwest Africa
	Central Africa. Equatorial Africa
.4	Angola
.5	Zaire. Congo (Democratic Republic)
.6	Equatorial Guinea
.7	Sao Tome e Principe
.8	French Equatorial Africa. French Congo
84.2	Gabon
.3	Congo (Brazzaville). Middle Congo
.4	Central African Empire. Central African Republic. Ubangi-Shari
.5	Chad
.6	Cameroon
	West Africa. West Coast
84.7	Benin. Dahomey
.8	Togo
85.2	Niger
.3	Ivory Coast
.4	Guinea
.5	Mali
.6	Upper Volta
.7	Senegal
.8	Mauritania
86.2	Nigeria
.3	Ghana
.4	Sierra Leone
.5	Gambia
.6	Liberia
.7	Guinea-Bissau. Portuguese Guinea
.8	Spanish Sahara
	Atlantic Ocean Islands
87.2	Bermuda
.3	Cape Verde Islands
.4	St. Helene
.5	Falkland Islands
	Indian Ocean Islands
88.2	Seychelles
.3	Comoro Islands
.4	Mauritius
.5	Reunion
90	Australia
97	New Zealand
	Pacific Ocean Islands
98.2	Trust Territory of the Pacific Including Mariana, Caroline and Marshall Islands
.3	Guam
.4	Papua New Guinea
.5	Solomon Islands
.6	Gilbert Islands Including Gilbert and Ellice Islands Colony
.7	Tuvalu
.8	New Caledonia

EXAMPLE 6, continued
_____

99.2	New Hebrides
.3	Fiji Islands
.4	Tonga
	Samoan Islands
.5	American Samoa
.6	Western Samoa

OBSERVE

1. The countries are listed in classified order.

2. Separation of the United States is typical.

3. Subarrangement for state serial reports is by successive cutter numbers.

4. Dedicated cutter numbers for subdivisions precede the country names under Other countries.

5. Each Other country has been assigned an individual class number.

6. Several places in the Tables of Geographical Divisions are not in the list. Among them are Monaco, Afghanistan, and Libya.

_____

In Example 6, under By state, A-W, the caption for .x has been changed to General serials and .x95 has been cancelled. Under Other countries, the caption for .A1-199 has been changed to General serials.

_____
EXAMPLE·7
_____

	Boards of trade, chambers of commerce, merchants' associations, etc.
	Cf. HF71+, Ministries, departments, etc.
HF 294	General works
	Including organization and works about boards of trade, etc., in general, in individual countries
295-343	Individual boards of trade, etc.
	For international boards of trade, etc., <u>see</u> HF294
	United States
295	State boards
296.A1-28	National boards of trade
.A29A-Z	Foreign-American boards of trade. By region or country, A-Z
	e.g. .A29B43 Chambre de commerce Belge aux Etats-Unis
.A3-Z	Cities, A-Z
298	Canada
299	West Indies, A-Z
300	Latin America. By region or country, A-Z

EXAMPLE 7, continued

302	Great Britain
304	Austria
306	France
308	Germany
	Including West Germany
310	Greece
312	Italy
314	Belgium
316	Netherlands
318	Soviet Union
320	Scandinavian countries, A-Z
322	Spain
323	Portugal
324	Switzerland
326	Balkan countries, A-Z
328	Other European regions or countries, A-Z
331	Asia. By region or country, A-Z
336	Africa. By region or country, A-Z
340	Australia
341	New Zealand
343	Pacific islands, A-Z

OBSERVE

A number of countries are listed without subordination to a larger geographical division.

Two other examples of countries listed without continents are HB101-123 (History of economics.   History of economic theory) and HD6460-6472 (Trade unions.   Labor unions. Workingmen's associations).   Note particularly the order of countries for HB101-123. The list. begins with Austria and Czechoslovakia; United States, Canada and Latin America follow Switzerland.

EXAMPLE 8

	Taxation. Administration and procedure
	Direct taxes (Special)
	Capitalization. Poll tax
	By region or country
	United States
HJ 4930	General works
4931	By region or state, A-Z

Other regions or countries.
Under each country:

I no.	Cutter no.	
.A2A-Z	.x	General works
.A3-Z	.x2	States, provinces, etc., A-Z

4932	Canada
.5	Latin America
4933	Mexico, West Indies, and Central America, A-Z
4934	South America. By region or country, A-Z
4935	Europe. By region or country, A-Z
4936	Asia. By region or country, A-Z
4937	Africa. By region or country, A-Z
4938	Australia
.5	New Zealand
4939	Pacific islands, A-Z

OBSERVE

1. Following the internal table, geographical divisions are printed in classified order.

2. A few countries are named and assigned class numbers.

3. Single class numbers represent continents and other areas.

4. By region or country, A-Z, provides for the cutter numbers of unlisted countries to be the first cutter number under the continental class numbers.

One of the more fully developed classified country listings occurs for HJ2360-3192.7 (Revenue and taxation). The class numbers HJ2360-2442 include a detailed treatment of the United States as a whole, followed by separate listings of the regions and the fifty states. Dedicated cutter-number sequences, one for regions and one for states, provide for subdivisions. Between HJ2449-HJ2889, the subdivisions for Canada, Latin America, and European countries are developed by class numbers in the schedule, dedicated cutter numbers, internal tables, and Subarranged like notes. Asia, Africa, island groups, Arctic and Antarctic regions, unlisted, are assigned to HJ2901-3192.7 (Other regions and countries) with a reference to the Tables of Geographical Divisions and an internal table.

ASSOCIATED COUNTRIES

In the Tables of Geographical Divisions and in schedule classified listings, countries associated together for one reason or another are grouped together. The connection among them may be political, economic, religious, etc.

The composition of some groups is made known in the Tables of Geographical Divisions and in schedule lists but there may be differences. Benelux countries, for example, in the Tables and at HE4811–4830.5 (Street railways) include three countries while only two are named in the schedule for HJ7820-7829 (Expenditure).

Other groups' membership is not identified. This class can be divided into two groups. Class numbers are examples of schedule assignments.

1. Associated countries in schedule enumerations and in the Tables of Geographical Divisions

HT1317	Arab countries
HJ8616	European Economic Community countries
HC499	Islamic countries

2. Associated countries in schedule enumerations only

HA1110-1116	Commonwealth of Nations
HA4021–4206	Communist countries
HC243.5	Council for Mutual Economic Aid
HD9698.4	European Atomic Energy Community
HC241.4	European Free Trade Association
HB130	Underdeveloped areas

Sometimes Communist countries or Underdeveloped areas or both apply to a subject when a Table of Geographical Divisions has been assigned. As neither of the two groups is among Table locations, provision for them is made after the internal table as shown at HG1495 and HG1496 (Money). Developing countries is the new name for Underdeveloped areas.

chapter 10
states

Extensive use is made of the state approach to subjects in Class H. States are a type of local geographical unit. The Tables of Geographical Divisions exclude states, with one exception. The central location column has a line for States, A-W, under the United States. This chapter considers provisions for the states of any country, the treatment of the states of the United States, and the states of other countries.

STATES OF ANY COUNTRY

Several different schedule situations provide for the states of any country. The situations may be grouped into the two basic geographical arrangements: alphabetical order and classified order.

Alphabetical Order of States

To obtain subdivision for the states of any country, a necessary accompaniment to the geographical authorization, By region or country, A-Z, is some form of subarrangement. The most common subarrangement for localities consists of a successive cutter-number pattern in which .x stands for General works and .x2 for Local, A-Z. Local, undefined, includes states. As usual for alphabetical order, the geographical divisions are not listed. A single class number would be assigned to By region or country, A-Z, preceding the Under each statement.

EXAMPLE I

Banking
    Special classes of banks and credit institutions
        Agricultural credit agencies

EXAMPLE 1, continued
_____

| HG 2041 | General works |
| 2051 | By region or country, A-Z |

Under each country:

.xA1-3	Periodicals. Societies. Serials
.xA6-Z	General works
.x2A-Z	By state, province, etc., A-Z

OBSERVE

1. A single class number is assigned to By region or country, A-Z.

2. Geographical divisions are not listed.

3. Combination successive cutter numbers and dedicated cutter numbers form the subarrangement for each country.

4. The subdivision for states and other local units is assigned to .x2.

5. Authorization for subdivision by state is made without the appellation Local.

6. The subarrangement follows the common pattern for localities in the order of its subdivisions. General works precedes Local.

_____

Classified Order of States

The standard division between enumeration in the schedule and the Tables of Geographical Divisions applies to the states of any country. Classified enumerations permit individual treatment of subordinate units under particular countries. The sections on States of the United States and States of Other Countries illustrate the treatment of states in enumerative display.

For the states of any country to be included when a Table of Geographical Divisions is designated, the Table must apply first to all countries. That means only Tables I-V. They are the only Tables in which the United States has range numbers. Second, Table V citations must be supplemented by some form of subarrangement for local development. Most frequently, an internal table is supplied. Conventional subdivisions, By state, A-Z, alone or with other types of localities and Local, A-Z, identified or unidentified by type, appear in the tables. The internal table for HQ1901-2030.7 (Women's clubs) has the subdivision By state, A-Z, set apart at a sequential number. Local is defined to include states in the internal table shown in Example 2.

EXAMPLE 2

Industry
The state and industrial organization
Inspection. Factory inspection
HD3661-3790.9   By region or country.   Table V[1]
Under each country:

4 nos.	1 no.	
(1)	.A1-4	Periodicals. Serials
(3)	.A6-Z4	General works
(4)	.Z5A-Z	Local: States, provinces, etc., A-Z

---

1. For Table V, see pp. 331-340 in H-HJ. Add country number in table to 3660.

OBSERVE

1. No countries are excluded.
2. The states for each country are to be included in the Local subdivision.

At HQ141-270.7 (Prostitution), provision for localities differs in the two-range columns. In the four-number column, sequential number (3) has been assigned to By state. In the one-number column, Local is at the fourth sequential indication. At HD5721-5851 (Labor market. Labor supply and demand), Table V is modified for the United States to provide especially for states.

STATES OF THE UNITED STATES

Subdivisions for the United States are frequently assigned class numbers in the schedule. Local development usually has a place among the subdivisions. Provision is made both for states individually and states collectively.

States Individually

There are four basic ways of requesting states individually: 1. by means of the instructions By state, A-W, and By region or state, A-Z; 2. by specifying Table of States II or III; 3. by listing the states alphabetically in the schedule; and 4. by the use of the Tables of Geographical Divisions. The first and second methods are discussed below.

States in the Table of States. The Table of States is composed of an alphabetical list of the fifty states and three columns labelled I, II, III. The District of Columbia has been deleted from the Table. Table I supplies a cutter number for each state. Table II furnishes each state with a single Arabic number. Table III allots two Arabic numbers to each state. The numbers in Tables II and III are not cutter numbers as such. The Table, appended to the schedule, saves repeating the names of the states in the schedule proper.

Table of States I, usually not cited, is to be used wherever the subdivision is By state, A-W, or By region or state, A-Z. Instructions may read otherwise, as at HG6133 in Example 3. A conflict between region and state cutter numbers does not occur because the series of dedicated cutter numbers in the Tables of Regions in the United States comes before Alabama's cutter number in Table of States I. Use the Table with Examples 3 and 8.

EXAMPLE 3

	Finance
	Lotteries
	By region or country
	United States
HG6126	General works
	Including history
6128	Policy
6133	State lotteries, A-W

OBSERVE

1. A single class number includes all states sponsoring lotteries.
2. States are to be cuttered from their initial letters.
3. A reference to Table of States I has not been made.
4. Using Tables of States I, the class number for lotteries run by the state of Oregon would be HG6133.O7.

Tables II and III are designed after the caption for state subdivision. The two Tables are to be used when so designated. Where either Table is to be employed, a range of class numbers is supplied. A footnote contains a base number, usually one less than the first number of the state range.

Table of States II provides numbers 1-52 for the states, with decimal extensions for Hawaii and numbers 8 and 15 omitted. Three references are made to Table II: HJ3871-3924 (Direct taxes (General)), HJ5023-5074 (Indirect taxes (General)) and HJ5323-5374 (Fees, licenses, stamp tax). Example 4 displays typical provisions for Table of States II.

EXAMPLE 4

Direct taxes (General)
By region or country
HJ 3871-3924   United States
3871   General works
3872-3924   States.   Tables of States II[1]

1. For Table of States II, see p. 344 in H-HJ. Add state number in table to 3872.

OBSERVE

1. A separate subdivision for States is provided.
2. A range of class numbers is assigned to the subdivision.
3. Table of States II is designated.

PROCEDURE

To apply Table II, add the number for the state from the Table to the base number in the footnote. The total becomes the class number for a work dealing with the subject in the state. The class number should fall within the limits of the spread of state numbers preceding the caption. Alabama and Wyoming are used with Example 4 to show that the class numbers fit into the range of numbers assigned to States.

Alabama
3872   The base number in the footnote
+ 1   The state number for Alabama in Table II
HJ3873   The class number for the subject in Alabama

Wyoming
3872   The base number in the footnote
+ 52   The state number for Wyoming in Table II
HJ 3924   The class number for the subject in Wyoming

The class number for the subject in Alabama matches the first number of the range assigned to States. The class number for Wyoming matches the last number of the range.

Table of States III provides odd numbers through 103 with a decimal extension for Hawaii and with numbers 15 and 29 omitted. Although only one number is printed for a state, there are actually two for each state, as the heading indicates and the footnote illustrates. Two numbers are supplied in an Under each subarrangement to pair with the two numbers for each state. Table of States III has been assigned to three sets of class numbers: HJ4183-4286 (Land use), HJ7551-7654 (Expenditure), and HJ9817-9920 (Public accounting). The Under each subarrangement for HJ7551-7654 has been revised to conform to those of HJ4183-4286, shown in Example 5 as illustrative of provisions for Table of States III.

EXAMPLE 5

<pre>
                          Direct taxes (Special)
                           Land tax. Real estate tax
                            By region or country
                             United States
    HJ4183-4286   States. Table of States III¹
                             Under each:
                               (1)   .A1-5   Periodicals. Societies.
                                                  Serials
                                        .A6-Z   General works
                               (2)   Special
                                                  For subarrangement, see
                                                   HJ4182
</pre>

1. For Table of States III, see p. 344 in H-HJ. Add state number in table to 4182.

OBSERVE

1. A range of numbers precedes States.
2. Numbers to add to the base number will be found for each state in Table of States III.
3. There are two numbers in the Under each provisions.
4. The base number is one less than the first number of the class-number range.

PROCEDURE

Except that the second class number must be ascertained, constructing class numbers with Table of States III is similar in procedure to that for Table of States II.

  1. For sequential number (1) in the Under each subarrangement
     a. Find the number for the state in the Table.
     b. Add the base number to the state number.

2. For sequential number (2)
    a. Add "I" to the first state number to form the second state number.
    b. Add the base number to the second state number.

Ohio is 73 in Table of States III. The second state number is 74. By the addition of 4182, the base number in the footnote for Example 5, to the state numbers, Ohio's numbers become HJ4255 and HJ4256. To each number, apply any other appropriate subarrangement such as dedicated cutter numbers. Cutter otherwise as required.

States Enumerated in the Schedule. When the names of the fifty states plus the District of Columbia are printed inthe schedule, commonly with some form of subarrangement, each state is assigned either a single class number or a span of numbers. Single class numbers are shown in Example 6 and spans in Example 7.

EXAMPLE 6

```
                    Penology
                       Documents
                          United States
                             Federal
HV 7245                         Serial
   7248                         Nonserial.  By date
                             State
                                Under each:

                                   .A1-5     Serial
                                   .A6       Nonserial.  By date
                                   .A7-Z     By place, A-Z
   7250                          Alabama
   7251                          Alaska
   7252                          Arizona
   7253                          Arkansas
   7254                          California
   7255                          Colorado, etc.
```

OBSERVE

1. One class number is assigned to each state.
2. Dedicated cutter numbers supply the subdivisions for each state.
3. By place means geographical units smaller than a state.

States in the Tables of Geographical Divisions. Coverage of the states can be achieved only when Tables I-V are referred to and the Table is not assigned to Other regions or countries. In addition, the phrase Except the United States may be a restriction. If one of the first four

Tables is designated, a number for states will be found in the Table. If Table V is designated, the four-number range allocated in it to the United States makes necessary a subarrangement with a subdivision for localities. Example 2 is representative. In it, countries are assigned to Table V without exception and the fourth sequential number represents the subdivision Local: states, provinces, etc., A-Z.

States Collectively and Confederate States

If states are provided for as a group under a subject, the provision precedes schedule numbers for individual states. The two examples show states treated collectively with and without subdivisions.

EXAMPLE 7

		Public finance
		Public credit. Debts. Loans
		By region or country
		United States
		States collectively
HJ	8223	General works
	8224	Special

```
                                          e.g.   Constitutional limitations, repudiation
         8225                       Early through 1860
         8227                       1861-
                              Regions
         8230                    New England and Atlantic states
         8235                    South
         8240                    Middle West
         8245                    Pacific States
                              States individually
                                 Under each:

                                 (0)    or    (5)      General works
                                 (1)          (6)      Special
                                                       History
                                 (2)          (7)         Early through 1860
                                 (3)          (8)         1860-1900
                                 (4)          (9)         1901-

         8250-8254            Alabama
         8255-8259            Alaska
         8260-8264            Arizona
         8265-8269            Arkansas
         8270-8274            California
         8275-8279            Colorado, etc.
```

OBSERVE

1. Collective provisions precede those for individual states.

EXAMPLE 7, continued

2. Subdivisions for states collectively have been given separate class numbers in the schedule.

3. Individual states are enumerated alphabetically following the collective provisions.

4. Each state has a range of five numbers.

5. Sequential numbers in the five-number double-column table match the state range numbers.

EXAMPLE 8

	Public finance
	Income and expenditure. The budget
	By region or country
HJ 2050-2052.5	United States
2052.A2	Periodicals, societies, etc.
	By state
2053.AI	Collective
.A2-W	By state, A-W

OBSERVE

1. States collectively and individually share the same class number.

2. States as a group are to be differentiated by the assignment of the dedicated cutter number .AI.

3. The states are not listed.

Another example of the separation of individual states from collective provisions is under the subject Taxation. The collective class number is HJ3258.A3-Z. The states are listed individually between HJ3260-3361.9. For subdivision, Table I is cited following the caption States individually. Note the Arabic number and also that the placement of the Table is a departure from the normal location of internal tables. The Table follows the enumeration of the states.

When appropriate, the Confederate States have been singled out and given separate treatment. HE6500 is the schedule number assigned to the Confederate States for Postal service.

STATES OF OTHER COUNTRIES

Unlike states of the United States, individual states of other countries are seldom identified by name in the schedule nor is there a table of states appended for other countries. States of other countries are handled by subdivision under the names of individual countries in schedule enumerations but much less frequently than for the United States. The phrase Other regions or countries is the usual instruction where separate arrangements for the United States have been made.

The four excerpts in Examples 9, 10, 11, and 12 feature classified enumerations wherein provisions for the states of countries are set forth by class numbers directly in the schedule. Alphabetical order for states is called for in Examples 9 and 10. Examples 11 and 12 display individual state names. States collectively have been provided for in only a few instances. One of those is shown in Example 13.

EXAMPLE 9

Public finance
Revenue. Taxation
By region or country
Mexico

HJ 2461	General works
	History. By period
2463	Early through 1810
2464	1810-1900
2466	1901-
2467	Special
2470	States, A-Z

OBSERVE

1.   A single class number has been assigned to the subdivision States, A-Z.
2.   The states are unlisted.
3.   The states are to be cuttered by their names.

EXAMPLE 10

Economic history and conditions
By region or country
America.   Western Hemisphere
Latin America

EXAMPLE 10, continued
_____

	South America
HC 186-190	Brazil
188	Regions, states, A-Z
189	Cities, A-Z

OBSERVE

1. Regions and states have been paired in one class number.

2. The order of the states is to be alphabetical.

_____

EXAMPLE 11
_____

Street railways.   Subways.   Rapid transit systems
    By region or country
        Other regions and countries
            Australia

HE 5161-5170	New South Wales
5171-5180	North Australia
5201-5210	Queensland
5211-5220	South Australia
5221-5230	Tasmania
5231-5240	Victoria
5241-5250	Western Australia

OBSERVE

The five continental states and Tasmania of the Commonwealth of Australia have been assigned class numbers in the schedule.

_____

EXAMPLE 12
_____

Classes arising from occupation
    Serfdom
        By region or country
            Germany

HT791	General works
795	Prussia
801	Other states, A-Z

EXAMPLE 12, continued
_____

OBSERVE

1. A former state of Germany has been named as a subdivision.

2. All other states are to be cuttered by their names under the same class number.

_____

EXAMPLE 13
_____

                    Public Credit. Debts. Loans
                      By region or country
                        Germany
        HJ 8650   General works
            8652   States collectively through 1871
            8654   Empire, 1871-
            8655   States, A-Z

OBSERVE

1. Through 1871, states are treated collectively.

2. Alphabetical order is assigned to individual states.

_____

In addition to state subdivision in the schedule under the names of individual countries, other techniques are employed. Examples 14 and 15 illustrate two different subarrangements.

EXAMPLE 14
_____

            Taxation. Administration and procedure
              Indirect taxes (General)
                By region or country
                  Other regions or countries
                  Under each country:

                  (1).A1-3   Periodicals. Societies. Serials
                                General works
                     .A7   Early works
                     .A8-Z   Recent works
                  (2)   States, provinces, etc., A-Z
                  For countries with one number, use .Z8A-Z for
                        States, provinces, etc.
        HJ 5075-5076   Canada

EXAMPLE 14, continued

<pre>
              Latin America
    5076.5   General works
5077-5078   Mexico
              Central America
    5079   General works
       .5   Belize
    5080   Costa Rica
</pre>

OBSERVE

1. Geographical divisions are listed with either one or two numbers.

2. An internal table supplies a sequential number for States, provinces, etc., for two-number countries.

3. A dedicated cutter number is assigned to States, provinces, etc., for one-number countries.

Where the geographical authorization is Other regions or countries, A-Z , and no countries are listed, provisions must be made for local subdivision. Example 15 shows such a provision.

EXAMPLE 15

<pre>
            Special classes of banks and credit institutions
              Pawnbroking
                By region or country
HG2106   Other regions or countries, A-Z
                    .x   General works
                    .x2   Policy
                    .x3   Local, A-Z
</pre>

OBSERVE

1. The unlisted countries are to be cuttered by their names.

2. Successive cutter numbers provide for subdivisions.

3. Local, A-Z, is without definition and includes states.

Because states of other countries do not appear in the Tables of Geographical Divisions, local development must take place elsewhere, most frequently in internal Tables. An internal table accompanying the citation of a Table of Geographical Divisions is shown in Example 16.

EXAMPLE 16

Lotteries
By region or country
HG6147-6270.9   Other regions and countries.   Table V[1]

4 nos.	1 no.	
(1)	.A2A-Z	General works
(3)	.A5-6	State, (provincial, etc.) lotteries, A-Z
(4)	.A7-Z	Other lotteries. By place, A-Z

---

1.   For Table V see pp. 331-340 in H-HJ. Add country number in table to 6140.

OBSERVE

1.   Table of Geographical Divisions V is cited.
2.   In the internal table, states are identified in a subdivision.

---

chapter 11
local

Subdivision by local entities is provided for under individual countries in schedule enumerations, in internal tables, in dedicated and successive cutter number sequences. The subarrangement pattern of successive cutter numbers which follows is widely used throughout the H schedule for local subdivision.

> By region or country, A-Z
> Under each country:
>
> .x   General works
> .x2   Local, A-Z

Assignment of a single class number to By region or country, A-Z, is customary. It is permissable to insert the subarrangement under the caption By region or country, A-Z, if the nature of the material makes local subdivision desirable.[1] Local has no defining terms and, therefore, covers local entities of any type. Certain kinds of local areas are characteristic of particular countries and that should be kept in mind when applying local subdivision. For example, cantons, counties, departments, parishes, and provinces are local units which need to be taken into account.

In classified enumerations, local subdivisions are supplied with class numbers in the schedule under individual countries. Where a Table of Geographical Divisions is assigned to By region or country, there must be an accompanying internal table or some other form of subarrangement to take care of local divisions that the Tables omit.

Types of localities to be included in Local may or may not be identified. In either case, alphabetical order is the general rule. Examples in this chapter are organized around three headings: Identified Localities; Unidentified Localities; and Cities, Counties, Provinces. Excerpts in the examples are from classified enumerations.

Examples I through 5 show the subdivision Local under names of countries accompanied by terms specifying the types of geographical units to be included. Examples 5 and 6 have been annotated with sample cutter numbers. Note that under Local finance, an inclusion note before HJ9000-9010 names counties, boroughs, communes, and municipalities.

EXAMPLE I

Economic history and conditions
By region or country
Europe
Switzerland
Local

HC 398	Regions and cantons, A-Z
399	Cities, A-Z

OBSERVE

1.   Under a country, three kinds of local units are named.

2.   Two local units are combined in one class number.

3.   "By" does not precede Regions and Cities.

EXAMPLE 2

Public finance
History and conditions
By region or country
Europe
France

HJ 1099	Local (Departments, provinces), A-Z
	.Z8 Colonies

OBSERVE

1.   Local is defined by two words in parentheses.

2.   A dedicated cutter number distinguishes a third local unit from other areas in the same class number.

EXAMPLE 3

Social history and conditions. Social problems. Social reform
   By region or country
      United States
         Local

HN 79
            By region or state, A-Z
               Subarranged like HC107
            Under each state:

               .x   General works
               .x2   By county, parish, or regions, A-Z
               .x3   Special topics (not otherwise provided
                      for), A-Z
80
       By city, A-Z

OBSERVE

1. The three types of local areas sharing the successive cutter number .x2 must be within the borders of a state of the United States.

2. By city has been given a separate class number.

EXAMPLE 4

Land use
   By region or country
      America
         United States
            Local

HD 207
              South
209
              West
210
              Other regions, A-Z
211
          By state, A-W
           By city, _see_ HD268, HD1291

OBSERVE

1. Regions, states, and cities of the United States are listed as local units.

2. Two regions and By state, A-W, have been given individual class numbers.

3. Subdivision By city has been assigned to other class numbers in the same subclass.

EXAMPLE 5

Economic history and conditions
By region or country
Europe
Great Britain
Local

HC 257   By region, country, etc., A-Z
e.g.   .N58   Northern Ireland
.S4   Scotland
.W3   Wales

258   By city, A-Z
e.g.   .L6   London

OBSERVE

1. Local has been defined at two class numbers.

2. Regions, countries, and cities are named as types of localities.

3. Etc. after country indicates that other local units are to be included in the class number.

4. By city has been given an individual class number and, therefore, is excluded from etc.

5. Sample cutter numbers have been provided at the two class numbers.

EXAMPLE 6

Utilization and culture of special classes of land
Water resources development. Water supply
By region or country
United States
States

HD 1694.A6-W   States
1695   Local (other than states), A-Z
e.g.   .A8   Arkansas River

OBSERVE

1. The words in parentheses bar the inclusion of one kind of local area in the local class number.

2. A river has been named as an example of a local unit.

In the Library of Congress Shelflist other types of local areas on catalog entries for HD1695 are valleys (Colorado River Valley), basins (Meremac Basin), and watersheds (Mill Creek Watershed).

While the word Local frequently precedes the defining areas, the word is not essential.

Phrases such as By region or state, By province, and By city regularly appear as subdivisions. Even By may be omitted.

UNIDENTIFIED LOCALITIES

The subdivision Local occurs frequently without any identifying geographical areas. Types of local units revealed in the preceding section are appropriate depending upon the country. Two extracts from the schedule, Examples 7 and 8, exemplify the use of Local wanting in definition.

EXAMPLE 7
___

```
                  Industrial concentration
                    Public utilities.  Public service commissions
                      By region or country
                        United States
HD 2766.A3A-Z             Periodicals.  Societies.  Serials
      .A6-Z               General works
   2767                   By region or state, A-Z
                            Under each state:

                              .x     Periodicals.  Serials
                              .x4    General works
                              .x5    Local, A-Z
   2768                   Other regions or countries, A-Z
                            Subarranged like HD2767
```

OBSERVE

1. Local areas are limited to geographical units within the borders of each state.
2. The Subarranged like note indicates that local units of other countries are to be treated in the same way as those of the United States.

EXAMPLE 8
___

```
                  Economic history and conditions
                    By region or country
                      Soviet Union
HC 337                  Local, A-Z
```

OBSERVE

1. Local applies to one country.

2.   The local areas of the country are represented by a single class number.

The instruction (not A-Z) is applied to Local at a successive cutter number under HJ2287 (Antiquities. Early forms). The non-alphabetical instruction means that localities are not to be represented in class numbers. An e.g. note shows the proper cuttering to be by country. Second cutter numbers are to be formed from main entries.

CITIES, COUNTIES, PROVINCES

Cities, counties, and provinces as types of localities are assigned under countries or states. It is exceptional for individual names of localities to be listed in the schedule. The term Local, unrestricted as to type, embraces cities and when they are appropriate to the country, counties, and provinces. Consistent with Local, subdivision for the three areas calls for alphabetical order in both classified enumerations and subarrangements which provide for local subdivision. Counties and cities are treated separately from provinces in the subsections which follow.

Cities and Counties

Cities are often set apart in a separate subdivision. The general practice is for subdivision by city to follow subdivision by state. For the United States, over 100 preassigned cutter numbers are available in the Table of Cities in the United States located at the end of each H volume. The Table is appropriately used whenever the subdivision under the United States is By city, A-Z. Cities of the United States are also provided for in the Tables of Geographical Divisions. Examples 9 through 11 show subdivision by city. The enumeration of cities by name in Example 11 is an unusual occurrence.

EXAMPLE 9
_____

Traffic engineering.   Roads and highways.   Streets
Traffic surveys (General)
By region or country
United States

HE 371.A2A-Z   Periodicals. Societies. Serials

EXAMPLE 9, continued

.A3A-Z	General works
.A4-Z	By region or state, A-Z
372	By city, A-Z
373	Other regions or countries

Under each country:

.x	General works
.x2	By region, state, etc., A-Z
.x3	By city, A-Z
e.g.	Soviet Union: .R9, General works; .R92A-Z, Provinces, etc., A-Z; .R93A-Z, Cities

OBSERVE

1. For both the United States and other countries, state subdivision precedes subdivision by city.

2. By city for the United States has been assigned a class number.

3. Cities of other countries are provided for in a successive cutter-number subarrangement.

4. An example of cuttering is given for other countries.

5. Subdivisions for localities are not preceded by Local.

EXAMPLE 10

	Local finance
	Including county, borough, commune, municipality, etc.
	Documents
HJ 9000-9010	General collections
	By region or country
	United States
9011.A1-4	General works
.A5-Z	By region or state, A-Z
9012	Counties, townships
	Arranged by state, A-W
9013	Cities, towns, A-Z

Under each:

a	Early documents
b	Main financial report
c	Auditor
d	Comptroller
e	Estimates, appropriations, etc.
g	Taxes and assessments
h	Commissioners of sinking fund
k	Board of supervisors
l	Local (Boroughs, etc.), A-Z

```
                                Canada
9014.A1-6                         General works
    .A7-Z                         Provinces
                                    Under each province:
                                        .x      General works
                                        .x2     Local, A-Z
9015-9099.6                     Other regions or countries
                                Subarranged like HJ15-99
                                Under each country:

                                  .A1-5     National documents
                                  .A55A-Z   By region or state, A-Z
                                  .A6-Z     By city
                                            Under each city:

                                              .A1+  General works
                                              .B1+  Budgets
                                              .C1+  Receipts and expenditures
                                              .D1+  Public debt
                                              .R1+  Administrative reports
                                              .S1+  Other.  Miscellaneous
```

OBSERVE

1. The inclusion note names several types of localities.

2. For both the United States and other countries, state subdivision precedes city subdivision.

3. There is one class number for countries and townships and one class number for cities and towns.

4. The Under each subarrangements provide for official publications to be represented in class numbers.

5. In the subarrangement for the United States, boroughs are named as a type of locality.

A different kind of subarrangement indication is seen in Example 10. The odd-appearing letter-number-plus combinations under By city for HJ9015-9099.6 bear a close resemblance to dedicated cutter numbers. The capital letters are to be placed in class numbers after the city cutter number to distinguish the several types of publications. The plus sign indicates that "one" can be expanded to accommodate the literature, e.g., between .A1-9, .B1-9, etc. In the geographical enumeration which Other regions or countries are to be subarranged like, Italy is HJ51. In Local finance, Italy is HJ9051. Three budget items for Rome could have these call numbers:

Italy	HJ9051	HJ9051	HJ9051
Rome	R6	R6	R6
Budgets	B126	B127	B128

The Under each subarrangement for the cities and towns of the United States in Example 10 has been revised to conform to the subarrangement for cities of other countries. The lower-case letters have been replaced by capital letters with 1+ added. Before the revision, the lower-case letters were placed in call numbers after the city cutter number. Then Arabic numbers were attached to the lower-case letters to indicate order of receipt. Four catalog entries in the Library of Congress Shelflist show the cutter numbers, publication letters, and order of receipt for the Minneapolis Comptroller's Department as .M6d, .M6d1, .M6d2, .M6d3.

EXAMPLE 11

```
                    Commerce
                      History
                        By period
                          Middle Ages (476-1400/1492)
                            By region or country
                              Italy
HF  411                        General works
    413                        Venice
    414                        Genoa
    415                        Pisa
    416                        Florence
    417                        Other  local,  A-Z
```

OBSERVE

1. Four cities are named in the schedule.

2. Unnamed local units are provided for alphabetically in one class number.

The history of urban groups and the city has two interesting city captions. International City (Projects) is at HT150 and Garden cities is found at HT161-165.

Subdivision by county is much less visible than by city in Class H. In classified listings, counties of countries other than the United States are usually included in Local, A-Z. Counties as a type are sometimes named under the United States in an Under each subarrangement. Example 12 shows one kind of subarrangement for counties of the States.

EXAMPLE 12

```
                    Freemasons
                      Directories and lists
   HS  381              General
                          By region or country
                            United States
       383                  General
       385                  By state, A-W
                              Under each:

                          .x    General works
                          .x2   Counties, etc.
```

OBSERVE

Counties of each state are provided for by successive cutter number.

Another example of provisions for counties of the United States is HV995 (Orphanages. Orphans) which is assigned to By city and county, A-Z. Counties and townships share HJ9012 (Local finance). An uncommon method of conveying subdivision by county is that of referring to a subdivision in an internal table. Just above HA221-227 (Statistical data. United States. Individual states), a see reference places counties in subdivision (7) of the ten-number column of the preceding internal table. In that table, subdivision (7) is By state, etc., A-Z. In the Tables of Geographical Divisions, counties appear only in the inclusion note for states under the United States.

Provinces

Provinces are often provided for specifically where they are typical geographical units of countries. Examples 13 and 14 reproduce sections of Class H which manifest treatment of provinces under individual countries.

EXAMPLE 13

```
              Public credit.  Debts.  Loans
                By region or country
                  Europe
                    Soviet Union
   HJ  8710             States, provinces, etc., A-Z
```

EXAMPLE 13, continued

OBSERVE

Provinces have been combined with other geographical areas in one class number.

EXAMPLE 14

```
                    Public finance
                      History and conditions
                        By region or country
                          Italy
                            Regions and provinces
    HJ  1187.8                Collective
                                Including grants-in-aid
        1188                  Individual, A-Z
```

OBSERVE

1. Regions and provinces are to be treated together.
2. Regions and provinces collectively and individually have been given separate class numbers.

Internal tables provide for the several types of localities. The most common single geographical subdivisions in internal tables are Local, A-Z, By state, A-Z, and By city, A-Z. There are also combinations of local units in one subdivision. These two combinations occur with the greatest frequency: By region or state, A-Z and By state, province, etc., A-Z. There can be more than one subdivision for localities in the same internal table. One example is HJ9550-9694.7 (Local finance) where separate sequential numbers are assigned to Provinces, states, regions, A-Z, and Cities, towns, etc., A-Z. HV6801-7220.5 (Crimes and criminal classes) has three local subdivisions: 1. Local, A-Z, for two-number countries; 2. By state, province, etc., A-Z, for ten-, five- and one-number countries; and 3. By place, A-Z, for ten- and five-number countries.

NOTES

1. Cataloging Service Bulletin 21:79 (Summer 1983).

chapter 12
other geographical divisions

The overall geographical direction, By region or country, includes some types of geographical divisions yet to be considered. They are examined in alphabetical order. As with all geographical subdivision, the extent of their inclusion differs from subject to subject.

COLONIES

Colonies must be accounted for in their time and place. Colonies are not represented in the Tables of Geographical Divisions; they do, however, merit places within the schedule proper. In the internal table for HE6651-7496 (Postal service), colonies are identified as local geographical units. In the internal table preceding HT1048-1050 (Slavery), the subdivision Colonies is independent of Local. There is a modification of the class numbers for France in a note for HF1761-2580.7 (Tariff policy (Protection and free trade)) to include its colonies.

CONTINENTS AND OTHER MAIN LAND AREAS

Continents, island groups, and the Arctic and Antarctic regions, along with America, form the first location level of the Tables of Geographical Divisions. Island groups are also discussed in a separate section. The numbers assigned to the areas in the Tables allow a classification number to be constructed when a Table is cited and a work dealing with the land form is at hand.

When a classified enumeration is limited primarily to continents and other main land areas, the variations are manifold. All of the geographical divisions involved may be listed, grouped with other areas in various combinations, or partially listed with some countries named. Generally, regions and countries are provided for alphabetically under the name of the continent. As the favored country, the United States is frequently the only country listed, often with its own subdivisions. For some enumerations, there is an Under each subarrangement applying to all divisions. Compare and contrast the continental displays and the treatment of their constituents in Examples 1, 2, and 3.

EXAMPLE 1

```
                          Societies
                            By region or country
                              Under each country:

                                  .A1-4   General works
                                  .A5-Z   Local, A-Z
          HS  61              United States
              63              Canada and other British America
              65              Other American countries, A-Z
              67              Great Britain
              71              Other European countries, A-Z
              81              Asia, A-Z
              84              Africa, A-Z
              87              Australia and New Zealand
              89              Pacific islands, A-Z
```

OBSERVE

1. The listing is in classified order.

2. Some countries have been given individual class numbers.

3. America is divided into three parts.

4. Europe is divided between Great Britain and other countries.

5. Australia and New Zealand share one class number.

6. Only one island group is listed.

7. A-Z means that constituent countries are to be cuttered by their names.

8. Subdivisions under each country are provided by the general subarrangement pattern in which Local follows General works.

EXAMPLE 2

```
                          Finance
                            By region or country
                              United States
          HG  181              General works
              183              By region or state, A-Z
              184              By city, A-Z
                            Other regions or countries
                              America
              185.A2           General works
                  .A3-Z        By region or country, A-Z
                              Europe
              186.A2           General works
                  .A3-Z        By region or country, A-Z
                              Asia
              187.A2           General works
                  .A3-Z        By region or country, A-Z
```

EXAMPLE 2, continued
_____

187.5	Africa
	.A2 General works
	.A3-Z By region or country, A-Z
	Atlantic Ocean Islands
188.A2	General works
.A3-Z	By island, A-Z
.5	Indian Ocean Islands
	.A2 General works
	.A3-Z By island, A-Z
189	Australia
.5	New Zealand
	Pacific Ocean Islands
190.A2	General works
.A3-Z	By island, A-Z
195	Underdeveloped areas

OBSERVE

1. The geographical divisions are in classified order.

2. The United States is treated apart from other American countries.

3. Class numbers have not been assigned directly to every geographical division.

4. There are separate class numbers for Australia and New Zealand.

5. Subdivisions are provided beneath geographical divisions.

6. One of the subdivisions is for General works.

7. Another subdivision is for constituent regions and countries, which are to be represented in call numbers by their cutter numbers.

_____

EXAMPLE 3
_____

	Radio. Wireless telegraph
HE 8675	General works
	By region or country
	United States
8677	Periodicals. Societies. Serials
8678	General works
8679	Other American regions or countries, A-Z
8680	Europe. By region or country, A-Z
8681	Asia. By region or country, A-Z
8682	Africa. By region or country, A-Z
8683	Other, A-Z

OBSERVE

1. The short list of geographical divisions is in classified order.
2. The United States is the only named country and the only area to which subdivisions with class numbers are assigned.
3. Regions and countries of the geographical divisions between HE8679-8682 are provided for alphabetically.
4. Unnamed geographical divisions are assigned to Other, A-Z.

ISLANDS

Single islands and groups of islands are geographical divisions in the schedule and the Tables of Geographical Divisions. Single islands are primarily those coextensive with countries. Greenland and Jamaica are examples. In addition, Martinique, the French Overseas Department and the island of the same name, and Australia, the continent and island of the same names are coterminous. The two islands, Mauritius, a country, and Reunion, a French Overseas Department, appear as constituents of the Indian Ocean Islands.

There are three large island groups presented as first-level locations in the Tables of Geographical Divisions: Atlantic Ocean Islands, Indian Ocean Islands, and Pacific Ocean Islands. Each island groups' components are listed in the central column. The components are groups of islands themselves with a few exceptions, some of which have been noted in the previous paragraph. In the schedule, the request for subarrangement by island may be for alphabetical order as in Examples 1 and 2 or constituents may be assigned individual class numbers as for HA2280-2295 (Statistical data, Atlantic Ocean Islands). Some other island groups, both in the schedule and in the Tables, are the Leeward Islands, Saint Pierre and Miquelon Island, and the Bahamas.

POSSESSIONS

Possessions as such are excluded from the Tables of Geographical Divisions but are in schedule enumerations under subjects to which they have relevance. Example 4 features a typical listing.

EXAMPLE 4

```
                    Clubs
                      By region or country
     HS  3125-3130       Africa
         3131-3135           British possessions
         3141-3145           French possessions
         3151-3155           German possessions  (Former)
              3165           Other African regions or countries, A-Z
```

OBSERVE

1. Possessions are listed under the continent in which they are located.

2. The identity of the possessions is made known only by the name of the controlling country in adjectival form.

TRUSTEESHIPS AND TERRITORIES

Of the eleven original trust territories established by the United Nations, only one remains as a trust territory -- the Trust Territory of the Pacific Islands.[1] In the Tables of Geographical Divisions and in classified enumerations, the Trust Territory is listed as a component of the Pacific Ocean Islands. An inclusion note at each entry of the Trust names its constituent island groups. In Table I, the Trust is 97.6 and one place in the schedule is HC681.5 (Economic history and conditions).

The Statesman's Yearbook lists Guam, Puerto Rico, American Samoa, and the Virgin Islands of the United States as Outlying Territories of the United States.[2] Guam and American Samoa are considered constituents of the Pacific Ocean Islands in the Tables of Geographical Divisions and in schedule enumerations, while Puerto Rico and the Virgin Islands are placed with the West Indies under Latin America. The subject Passenger traffic (General), By region or country, has the class number HE212 for Outlying territories (General) of the United States.

The French Territory of the Afars and Issas, once an overseas territory of France, has become the Republic of Djibouti.[3] The Republic's former name appears in the Tables and the schedule under Northeast Africa. HE5118 (Street railways) represents the Territory in the schedule.

There are other territories, but they have a minor place in Class H geographical subdivision. The Commonwealth of Australia, for example, has two territories, only one of which is included when the Commonwealth's constituents are enumerated in the schedule. The Australian Capital Territory is omitted between HE3461-3500 (Railways). Similarly, the Canadian Yukon Territory and Northwest Territories have a place only when the instruction calls for provinces alphabetically.

NOTES

1. Statesman's Yearbook; Statistical and Historical Annual Data for 1983-1984, 120th ed. (New York: St. Martin's Press, 1983), p. 6.
2. Ibid., pp. 1554-1564.
3. Ibid., p. 414.

part three
appendix

tables of geographical divisions: geographical divisions arranged alphabetically with table I numbers

Every place name in the central column of the tables is listed. Includes additions and changes through March 1984. Names are given in the form in which they are listed in the Tables.

TABLE I - GEOGRAPHICAL DIVISIONS

68.7	Aden (Colony and Protectorate)	24.5	Bahamas
69.6	Afghanistan	68.9	Bahrein
82	Africa	64	Balkan States
64.5	Albania	71.6	Bangladesh
82.4	Algeria	84.7	Basutoland
I	America	84.9	Bechuanaland
98.7	American Samoa	53	Belgium
61.3	Andorra	17.5	Belize
85.4	Angola	52	Benelux countries
100	Antarctic regions	86.7	Benin
81.5	Arab countries (Collective)	88.53	Bermuda
68.55	Arabia	71.3	Bhutan
68.55	Arabian Peninsula	84.9	Botswana
99	Arctic regions	32	Bolivia
31	Argentina	33	Brazil
68	Asia	86	Brazzaville
	Atlantic Ocean Islands	37.3	British Guiana
	precedes 88.5	17.5	British Honduras
89	Australia	83.2	British Somaliland
47	Austria	28.5	British West Indies
88.5	Azores	74.3	Brunei

TABLE I, Geographical Divisions, continued

65	Bulgaria	36	Ecuador
69.7	Burma	82.7	Egypt
83.8	Burundi	44	England
		85.3	Equatorial Africa
73.3	Cambodia	85.6	Equatorial Guinea
86.4	Cameroon	83	Ethiopia
15	Canada	42	Europe
88.6	Canary Islands	42.8	European Economic Community countries
88.63	Cape Verde Islands		
24	Caribbean area		
97.6	Caroline Islands	88.73	Falkland Islands
85.3	Central Africa	76.5	Far East
86.2	Central African Republic	98.5	Fiji Islands
17	Central America	55.3	Finland
7	Central States	80	Formosa
69.8	Ceylon	48	France
86.3	Chad	85.8	French Congo
34	Chile	85.8	French Equatorial Africa
78	China	37.7	French Guiana
35	Colombia	72	French Indochina
88.83	Comoro Islands	86.6	French-speaking West Africa
86	Congo (Brazzaville)	29.5	French West Indies
85.5	Congo (Democratic Republic)	83.3	French Territory of the Afars and Issas
18	Costa Rica		
25	Cuba	85.9	Gabon
68.3	Cyprus	88	Gambia
47.3	Czechoslovakia	49	Germany
		87.8	Ghana
86.7	Dahomey	61.5	Gibraltar
57	Denmark	97.9	Gilbert Islands
83.3	Djibouti	43	Great Britain
26.5	Dominican Republic	8	Great Lakes region
37.5	Dutch Guiana	67.5	Greece
29.3	Dutch West Indies	99.5	Greenland
		29.7	Guadeloupe
76.5	East Asia	97.7	Guam
49.5	East Germany		

TABLE I, Geographical Divisions, continued

19	Guatemala	73.4	Laos
37	Guianas	15.5	Latin America
87.2	Guinea	68.4	Lebanon
88.3	Guinea-Bisseau	28.7	Leeward Islands
37.3	Guyana	84.7	Lesotho
		88.2	Liberia
26	Haiti	82.6	Libya
13	Hawaii	47.9	Leichtenstein
20	Honduras	52	Low countries
81	Hongkong	54.5	Luxembourg
47.5	Hungary		
		79	Macao
58	Iceland	84.2	Madagascar
71	India	88.55	Madeira Islands
88.74	Indian Ocean Islands	84.2	Malagasy Republic
72	Indochina	85	Malawi
75	Indonesia	73.6	Malaya
69.2	Iran	73.6	Malaysia
69	Iraq	88.75	Maldive Islands
46	Ireland	87.3	Mali
46	Irish Republic	51.5	Malta
81.7	Islamic countries (Collective)	97.6	Mariana Islands
68.45	Israel	97.6	Marshall Islands
83.2	Italian Somaliland	29.9	Martinique
51	Italy	87.6	Mauritania
87	Ivory Coast	88.85	Mauritius
		16	Mexico
27	Jamaica	5	Middle Atlantic States
77	Japan	86	Middle Congo
68.5	Jordan	68.2	Middle East
		5	Middle States
73.3	Kampuchea	9	Mississippi Valley
83.5	Kenya	48.5	Monaco
88.93	Kerguelen Islands	77.8	Mongolian People's Republic
77.5	Korea	82.3	Morocco
68.95	Kuwait	84	Mozambique
		68.75	Muscat and Oman

85.2	Namibia	7	Plains States
68.2	Near East	55.7	Poland
69.9	Nepal	62	Portugal
54	Netherlands	88.3	Portuguese Guinea
29.3	Netherlands Antilles	28	Puerto Rico
98.3	New Caledonia		
4	New England	68.85	Qatar
98.4	New Hebrides		
97.5	New Zealand	88.9	Reunion
21	Nicaragua	84.5	Rhodesia
86.9	Niger	II	Rocky Mountain region
87.7	Nigeria	67	Romania
82.2	North Africa	55	Russia
2	North America	83.7	Rwanda
77.6	North Korea (Democratic People's Republic)		
		88.65	St. Helena
82.9	Northeast Africa	15.25	Saint Pierre and Miquelon Islands
4	Northeastern States	85.7	Sao Tome e Principe
45.5	Northern Ireland	23	Salvador
84.6	Northern Rhodesia		Samoan Islands precedes 98.7
II	Northwestern States	51.3	San Marino
59	Norway	26.5	Santo Domingo
85	Nyasaland	68.6	Saudi Arabia
		56	Scandinavia
68.75	Oman	45	Scotland
77.8	Outer Mongolia	87.5	Senegal
		88.8	Seychelles
97.55	Pacific Ocean Islands	87.9	Sierra Leone
12	Pacific States	74	Singapore
71.5	Pakistan	98	Solomon Islands
68.45	Palestine	83.2	Somalia
22	Panama	84.4	South Africa
22.5	Panama Canal Zone	30	South America
97.8	Papua New Guinea	69.3	South Asia
38	Paraguay	77.5	South Korea
39	Peru	83.4	Southeast Africa
76	Philippine Islands	72	Southeast Asia

TABLE I, Geographical Division, continued

84.3	Southern Africa		68.8	United Arab Emirates
84.5	Southern Rhodesia		82.7	United Arab Republic
6	Southern States		3	United States
68.7	Southern Yemen		87.4	Upper Volta
85.2	Southwest Africa		40	Uruguay
10	Southwestern States			
55	Soviet Union		41	Venezuela
61	Spain		73.5	Vietnam
88.4	Spanish Sahara		28.3	Virgin Islands of the United States
69.8	Sri Lanka			
82.8	Sudan		44	Wales
37.5	Surinam		86.5	West Africa
84.8	Swaziland		86.5	West Coast
60	Sweden		49	West Germany
63	Switzerland		24	West Indies
68.35	Syria		1	Western Hemisphere
			98.8	Western Samoa
80	Taiwan		28.9	Windward Islands
83.9	Tanganyika			
83.9	Tanzania		68.7	Yemen (People's Democratic Republic)
73.55	Thailand			
86.8	Togo		68.65	Yemen (Yemen Arab Republic)
98.6	Tonga		65.5	Yugoslavia
29	Trinidad and Tobago			
88.7	Tristan de Cunha		85.5	Zaire
68.8	Trucial States		84.6	Zambia
97.6	Trust Territory of the Pacific		83.9	Zanzibar
82.5	Tunisia		84.5	Zimbabwe
68.25	Turkey			
86.2	Ubangi-Shari			
83.6	Uganda			

bibliography

Arick, Mary Catherine. "Subclassification and Book Numbers of Documents and Official Publications." In The Use of the Library of Congress Classification; Proceedings of the Institute on the Use of the Library of Congress Classification. Edited by Richard H. Schimmelpfeng and C. Donald Cook. Chicago: American Library Association, 1968.

Bain, J. Paul. "The Use of the Tables in the Library of Congress Classification." In Mildred H. Downing, Introduction to Cataloging and Classification. 5th ed. Jefferson, N.C.: McFarland and Co., 1981.

_____. "The Use of the Tables in the Library of Congress Classification: Schedules H and P." In Mildred H. Downing, Introduction to Cataloging and Classification. 5th ed. Jefferson, N.C.: McFarland and Co., 1981.

Bead, Charles C. "The Library of Congress Classification: Development, Characteristics, and Structure." In The Use of the Library of Congress Classification; Proceedings of the Institute on the Use of the Library of Congress Classification. Edited by Richard H. Schimmelpfeng and C. Donald Cook. Chicago: American Library Association, 1968.

Cataloging Service Bulletin. Washington, D.C.: Library of Congress, Processing Services, 1-21. Summer, 1978-Spring, 1984.

Chan, Lois Mai. Cataloging and Classification: An Introduction. Library Education Series. New York: McGraw-Hill, 1981.

_____. Immroth's Guide to the Library of Congress Classification. Library Science Text Series. 3rd ed. Littleton, Colo.: Libraries Unlimited, 1980.

Class H, Social Sciences, Subclasses H-HJ: Economics; Library of Congress Classification Schedules, A Cumulation of Additions and Changes Through 1981. Detroit: Gale Research Company, 1982.

Class H, Social Sciences, Subclasses H-HJ: Economics; Library of Congress Classification Schedules, A Cumulation of Additions and Changes Through 1982. Detroit: Gale Research Company, 1983.

Class H, Social Sciences, Subclasses HM-HX: Sociology; Library of Congress Classification

Schedules, A Cumulation of Additions and Changes Through 1981. Detroit: Gale Research Company, 1982.

Class H, Social Sciences, Subclasses HM-HX: Sociology; Library of Congress Classification Schedules, A Cumulation of Additions and Changes Through 1982. Detroit: Gale Research Company, 1983.

Grout, Catherine W. Explanation of the Tables Used in the Schedules of the Library of Congress Classification, Accompanied by an Historical and Explanatory Introduction. New York: Columbia University, School of Library Service, 1940.

Hedlesky, Nicholas. "Special Problems in Social and Political Sciences (Classes H and J)." In The Use of the Library of Congress Classification; Proceedings of the Institute on the Use of the Library of Congress Classification. Edited by Richard H. Schimmelpfeng and C. Donald Cook. Chicago: American Library Association, 1968.

Herrick, Mary Darrah. "Orientation of Staff and Clientele into the Library of Congress Classification In The Use of the Library of Congress Classification; Proceedings of the Institute on the Use of the Library of Congress Classification. Edited by Richard H. Schimmelpfeng and C. Donald Cook. Chicago: American Library Association, 1968.

Hoage, A. Annette Lewis. The Library of Congress Classification in the United States: A Survey of Opinions and Practices, with Attention to Problems of Structure and Application. D.L.S. dissertation, Columbia University, 1961.

Immroth, John P. "Library of Congress Classification." Encyclopedia of Library and Information Service, 15:93-200. New York; Marcel Dekker, 1975.

International Geographic Encyclopedia and Atlas. Boston: Houghton Mifflin, 1979.

LaMontagne, Leo E. American Library Classification with Special Reference to the Library of Congress Classification. Hamden, Conn.: Shoe String Press, 1961.

Manheimer, Martha L. Cataloging and Classification: A Workbook. 2nd ed. rev. and exp. New York: Dekker, 1980.

Statesman's Year-book; Statistical and Historical Annual Data for 1983-1984. 120th ed. New York: St. Martin's Press, 1983.

U.S. Library of Congress. Subject Cataloging Division. Classification, Class H, Subclasses H-HJ, Social Sciences: Economics. 4th ed. Washington, D.C.: Library of Congress, 1981.

_____. Classification. Class H, Subclasses HM-HX, Social Sciences: Sociology. 4th ed. Washington, D.C.: Library of Congress, 1980.

_____. L.C. Classification--Additions and Changes, Lists 209-213, January, 1983-March, 1984. Washington, D.C.: Library of Congress, 1983-1984.

_____. The Library of Congress Shelflist. Microfiche ed. Ann Arbor: University Microfilms International, 1978-1979.

Wynar, Bohdan S. Introduction to Cataloging and Classification. 6th ed. with the assistance of Arlene Taylor Dowell and Jeanne Osborn. Littleton, Colo.: Libraries Unlimited, 1980.

index

A and Z cutter numbers. <u>See</u> Dedicated
   cutter numbers.
Alphabetical arrangement of topics.
   <u>See also</u> Countries; Geographical arrangements; Localities; Regions not limited to
   one country; States of any country;
   United States (States).
   and classified order, 67-68, 95-96
   contrasted to non-alphabetical order, 7
   false, 9, 34-37
   in internal tables, 8, 11
   named in the schedule, 7-8
   under General Special, 53
   use required, 7
   unnamed in the schedule, 9-11
Arctic and Antarctic regions, 62, 83, 125
Associated countries, 75, 96-97

Base numbers, 56, 63
   multiple, in footnote, 58-59
   procedure for applying, 56-57
   procedure for applying with Tables of
      States II, 103
   procedure for applying with Tables of
      States III, 104-105
   procedure for applying with Tables of
      Geographical Divisions, 57-58, 64-66

Cities, 118-120. <u>See also</u> United States.
   in countries other than the United States,
      121
   procedure for applying letters of the alpha-
      bet to subtopics, 120-121
Classified arrangement of geographical divi-
   sions. <u>See</u> Geographical arrangements.
Colonies, 125
Communist countries, 97
Confederate States, 107
Continents, 125-128

omitted from classified lists in the schedule,
   87, 94-95
Counties. <u>See also</u> United States.
   other than United States, 121
Countries. <u>See also</u> United States.
   alphabetical arrangement, 85-87
   alphabetical and classified arrangement,
      95-96
   associated, 75, 96-97
   classified lists in the schedule, 85, 87, 89-94
   continents omitted preceding, 94-95
   extent of range numbers, known by, 41, 87
   features of subdivision, 85
   in Tables of Geographical Divisions, 62, 87-
      89
   Library of Congress successive cutter numbers
      for (selected), 33
   Table of Regions and Countries in One Alpha-
      bet, 85-86
Cutter numbers. <u>See</u> Dedicated cutter numbers;
   Successive cutter numbers.

Dedicated cutter numbers
   and Tables of Geographical Divisions, 20-21
   as second cutter numbers, 19-20
   characteristics, 15-16
   directions in a note, 18-19
   in internal tables, 21-22, 42
   in Table of Regions in the United States, 21
   Library of Congress call numbers (selected),
      17, 33, 60
   notation, 15
   procedure for applying, 17-18
   successive cutter numbers with, 19-20
   use required, 15
District of Columbia
   deleted from Table of States, 102
   excluded from internal table provisions, 48
Divided like note. <u>See</u> Subarranged like note.

Special purpose cutter numbers. See Dedicated cutter numbers.
States of any country
  alphabetical arrangement, 99-100
  Tables of Geographical Divisions, handling with, 100-101
States of countries other than the United S States
  collectively, 110
  in classified lists in the schedule, 108-111
  Tables of Geographical Divisions, handling with, 112
States (U.S.). See United States (States).
Subarranged like note, 23-26
  model numbers, 23
  procedure for applying, 26-27
Subdivision, definition, 2
Subdivisions in internal tables, 41
Successive cutter numbers
  alphabetical arrangement in appearance, 9, 34-37
  dedicated cutter numbers with, 19-20
  in internal tables, 32-34, 42, 95-96
  Library of Congress numbers (selected), 33, 38, 39
  localities, standard subarrangement for, 113
  notation, current, 29-31
  notation variations, 34-39
  procedure for applying, 31-32

Table of Cities in the United States, 56-60, 118
Table of Regions and Countries in One Alphabet, 59-60, 73, 85-86
Table of Regions in the United States, 21, 79-80, 102
Table of States, 101-102
Table of States I, 59-60, 79, 102
Table of States II, 56, 102-103
  procedure for applying, 103
Table of States III, 56, 102, 104
  procedure for applying, 104-105
Tables of Geographical Divisions. See also Countries; Localities; Regions not limited to one country; States of any country; States of countries other than the United States; United States.
  additions and changes to, 63
  Arctic and Antarctic regions in, 62, 83, 125
  associated countries in, 96-97
  base numbers with, 56-59, 63
  characteristics, 62-63
  continents in, 62, 125
  dedicated cutter numbers with, 20-21

index to, 133-137
internal tables with, 21-22, 41, 57-58, 64-66, 112
islands in, 62, 128
modified, 66-67, 125
procedure for applying, no internal table, 56-57, 63-64
procedure for applying with internal table, 57-58, 64-66
trusteeships and territories in, 129
Tables of Subdivisions under Industries and Trades, 9, 34-37
Territories. See Trusteeships and territories.
Topical cutter numbers. See Alphabetical arrangement of topics.
Tropics, 83
Trusteeshlps and territories, 129

Underdeveloped areas, 97
Under each statement, 41
United States. See also District of Columbia; Metropolitan areas.
  cities, provision for in Tables of Geographical Divisions, 62, 118
  Cities, Table of, 59-60, 118
  counties, 121-122
  "except for the United States" direction, 48, 67
  in Tables of Geographical Divisions I-V only, 62, 100-101, 105-106
  metropolitan areas, 78
  regions larger than a state in Tables of Geographical Divisions, 80
  regions within a state, 81
  separation from other countries in classified lists, 48, 76, 85
  Table of Regions in the United States, 21, 79-80, 102
  Territories of, provision for, 129
United States (States)
  alphabetical lists in the schedule, 105-106
  collectively, 106-107
  Confederate States, 107
  Library of Congress successive cutter numbers for (selected), 38, 39
  Regions within, 81
  Table of States, 101-102
  Tables of States I, 56-60, 79, 102
  Tables of States II, 56, 102-103
  Tables of States III, 56, 102, 104-105
  Tables of Geographical Divisions, provision for in, 62, 105-106
"unless otherwise provided for" direction, 47-48, 67

143

unnec. ?

120
119